SHOTS HEARD ROUND THE WORLD

An Ambassador's Hunting Adventures on Four Continents

SHOTS
HEARD
ROUND THE WORLD

An Ambassador's Hunting
Adventures on Four Continents

ELLIS O. BRIGGS

ILLUSTRATED BY RUDOLF FREUND

NEW YORK · THE VIKING PRESS · 1957

PUBLISHED IN 1957 BY THE VIKING PRESS, INC.
AT 625 MADISON AVENUE, NEW YORK 22, N.Y.

PUBLISHED IN CANADA BY
THE MACMILLAN COMPANY OF CANADA LIMITED

Acknowledgment is made to *The Saturday Evening Post,* in which "Animal Interlude—with Bears" appeared under the title "My Tangle with the President's Bears"; *Sports Illustrated,* which published "How to Shoot Non-Communist Pheasants in Czechoslovakia"; *House & Garden* for "The Pheasants of Cheju Island"; and *Foreign Service Journal* for "The Biggest Frog in the World."

LIBRARY OF CONGRESS CATALOG CARD NUMBER: 57-9492
PRINTED IN THE UNITED STATES OF AMERICA

FOR LUCY

Contents

Although most of the drawings require no explanation, iden-
tification of the following may be of interest to the reader:
title page, Falkland kelp geese; page 27, pepper bird, West
African fiscal shrike (*Lanius collaris Smithii*); page 32,
mamba; page 38, gray-breasted helmet guinea fowl
(*Numida meleagris*); page 41, upland geese;
page 112, Korean wild swans.

SHOTS HEARD ROUND THE WORLD

*An Ambassador's Hunting
Adventures on Four Continents*

Foreword

THESE TALES are dedicated to the American Foreign Service, which has been my home away from home for over thirty years. Although the stories span a generation from my service as vice consul in Callao to my appointment as ambassador to Brazil, they were written during the last two years, mostly in Korea and Peru, between *kimchi* dinners in the shadow of North Mountain and late banquets beside Pizarro's Rimac, with pisco sours at eleven p.m. and *corbina escabechada* following after. Add those exposures to a busy Chancery day, and the schedule doesn't provide much leeway for meditation over a typewriter—an observation I made from time to time to the patient executives of the Viking Press, whose optimistic belief that a wider audience now awaits I hope is not misplaced.

The unpredictable irregularity of Foreign Service life is one of its distinguishing characteristics. The notion persists, nourished by certain gentlemen who write inside-dope newspaper columns and cartoonists, that professional diplomats are insatiable party-goers. This has its origin in the fact that diplomats are required to attend innumerable official functions, and whenever Bulganin upends a tumbler with Chip Bohlen there is a photographer lurking behind a potted palm to record the event for posterity. But the corollary conclusion—that diplomats approach parties with the effervescent enthusiasm of the liberated bubbles in the bad champagne they are invited to consume—is highly suspect among the corps of professional officers who transact Uncle Sam's business in far places.

Experience demonstrates that a prime ingredient in the ability to conduct affairs is personal confidence, which in

turn derives, as it does in business at home, from relationships among individuals. Those relationships are facilitated
among foreign officials by social affairs and the relaxed at-
mosphere of a party: you can save a great deal of time by
stopping the minister of public works beside an oleander
bush in somebody's garden and asking him if it's true his
government plans to dam the Pongo de Manseriche, instead
of having your secretary call his secretary and make an appointment to ask the same question with his office desk between you.

But as to parties per se, I have yet to encounter the Foreign Service officer worth his name on the next promotion
list who regards them as much more than adjuncts to the
performance of official duties—adjuncts often useful but not
infrequently of a harrowing and repetitious boredom. And
as for the striped pants in which according to legend we are
supposed to conduct our magic enterprises, let my own experience enlighten the record. During the past decade, com-
prising service at four capitals, I have worn my cutaway
and striped trousers on only two occasions: first when I presented my credentials to President Batlle Berres of Uruguay,
and again in 1955 when I rode in the elegant vice-regal car-
riage to the Palacio Presidencial in Lima. I said *my* cutaway
advisedly, for there was a third occasion, painful to recall,
in Prague. I was scheduled to call at Hradcany Castle,
where Klement Gottwald, who later gave an impressive
demonstration of "communist emulation" by electing rigor
mortis within ten days of the demise of Comrade Stalin, was
to receive the new American ambassador at ten-thirty a.m.
An hour before the event I discovered that the trunk in
which I thought I had packed my cutaway contained instead my hunting clothes. I discovered further that the trunk
in which my cutaway nested among its mothballs was still
somewhere en route, between Montevideo and Bohemia.

Deeming it inexpedient to greet my first communist chief

of state in *bombachas,* I presented President Truman's letter
of credence to President Gottwald wearing the hastily assembled coat of the American consul and the trousers of the
third secretary, who were accordingly deprived of the privilege of attending my investiture, and I carried a beat-up
high hat that Hedda, the housekeeper in the embassy residence, found in a closet. The bonnet probably belonged to
one of the Petcheks, who built the house in the 1920s. Anyway, the consul was a large and portly man and his coat
fitted me as though tailored by Omar the Tentmaker. When
I stood straight in it there seemed to be a watermelon con-
cealed on my stomach and the general effect was that of a
Slovak matron who ought to be taking off at top speed for
the nearest socialized maternity clinic. I delivered my address to President Gottwald leaning sharply backward, to
keep the front of the consul's coat from swinging eight
inches away from the belt buckle holding up the third secretary's trousers, and pictures taken that November morning give the impression that the new ambassador is about
to tip into the supporting arms of his air attaché and his
counselor of embassy, standing behind him.

And in Korea, in 1952, that fine patriot President Rhee
received me in a business suit, in his devastated capital of
Seoul, and sent word for me likewise to wear one. Syngman
Rhee told me afterward that he lost *his* cutaway when the
Communists boiled across the thirty-eighth parallel in June
of 1950, capturing his capital. "Only favor the Communists
ever did me," remarked the venerable president.

These stories won't tell ambitious young men how to get
into the Foreign Service. That information, in the kind of
prose that emanates from the Potomac reaches, is contained
in a bulletin obtainable from The Secretary of State, Washington 25, D.C. That document convinces me that I was
fortunate to have entered the service in 1925, before the
present examinations were invented. Nowadays, upon pre-

senting satisfactory evidence of eligibility, an applicant is designated to take the written examinations. Subsequently those who pass are invited to appear, one at a time, before an oral board. Having surmounted that hurdle, your case is "processed" with a "full field check" and you are in due course admitted to fellowship as a Foreign Service Officer, Class VIII, and after the completion of a specialized training program at the Department of State you are sent abroad as a fledgling vice consul.

A generation ago things went faster. Batches of five nervous candidates were questioned immediately after the written examinations. Four applicants sat on a bench and perspired, each hoping the examiners wouldn't run out of easy questions before it was his turn, while the fifth was sharply examined. It was a tense ordeal, but quickly over, and if the ensuing letter from the State Department was addressed to J. Sediment Peachpit, *Esquire* (instead of Mister), you were in, and you shortly had a commission in your pocket and a diplomatic passport in your hand as you went up the gangway.

Those examinations remind me that I recently asked Professor Arnold Toynbee, who was in Peru studying Andean civilizations, why it was the Incas had no wheel. The Incas built temples defying time, and their irrigation ditches are marvels of twentieth-century engineering. The Incas were bright as buttons, I declared to the professor. They built enduring highways in the Andes—but they had no wheels. Why was that? I asked Dr. Toynbee.

The professor is one of the wisest of living men. He considered the problem. "Wheels," he said, and then, after cogitation. "The Incas had no wheels because they didn't invent them. If that answers your question . . ." He thought some more and remarked, "The Incas didn't know about buttons either."

I doubt if the professor's explanation would make a favorable dent in the present process of "screening" Foreign Service candidates but, fortunately for me in 1925, no one thought to ask me that question. What they did ask me was to comment on the differences between British and French colonial policy in the postwar period (meaning post World War I), and who-what-where-or-when Novorossisk was. I found out later that the who-what-where-or-when questions were booby traps, to find out whether a candidate, who wasn't expected to know the answer, would reply, "I don't know, sir" (which was the correct answer), or whether he would flounder around trying to impress his tormentors by inventing something irrelevant but plausible to conceal his ignorance.

On the British and French I murmured nervously about implanting among backward people the notion of abstract justice, versus Gallic paternalism, and I mentioned colonialism as an emerging world issue (a fine understatement as I look back thirty years upon it), but I knocked Novorossisk for a loop because I once took a trip on a Black Sea freighter and in a water-front bistro in that unsavory port, while I sampled the vodka, a Ukrainian soldier stole my watch. The incident rankled, and by way of getting even with Novorossisk I told the oral board what I thought of that city in several uncomplimentary sentences. The board was possibly surprised but all I had for my Novorossisk triumph was a thin smile from Francis White, now our ambassador to Mexico, who countered by asking me about the Treaty of Turkmanchai. Francis knew about Turkmanchai from having served in Persia, but I hadn't—and didn't.

So I was glad to have entered the Foreign Service before the present examinations were conceived. Today's entrance requirements make mine look like a taxi ride from Georgetown to Foggy Bottom compared to negotiating for a safari to the edge of the Mau Mau country. If these stories of the Foreign Service have some of the flavor of my lighter activities, or if they recapture the spell of living at fifteen posts in thirty-one years, I shall be content.

I enjoy the Foreign Service because of the infinite variety of the tasks it imposes, and because of the challenge and the pride of transacting our government's business abroad. From Liberia to Czechoslovakia, and from Brazil to Korea, there are no two posts alike. There are no Foreign Service chores, from the vice consul's issuing a visa or taking a marine note of protest against damage done by "the winds and waves and billows of the sea," to an ambassador's negotiating an important treaty, that are dull or unrewarding. But I admire the Foreign Service chiefly for the fine men and women who are in it; for the unpublicized work that they do day by day on behalf of our government, and for the staunch and cheerful way in which they do it. These loyal Americans have been my companions and my friends, and I am proud to be associated with them.

The Foreign Service is cherished for an additional reason. Now and then, during a lull in affairs, or when some agency in Washington wants to know how a remote irrigation project financed by the Export-Import Bank is progressing, there is time out for hunting or fishing. There is a good deal of that in these pages.

These stories have been written by me in my personal capacity and on my own responsibility, though they have been read in the Department of State.

President Rhee's bears, by the way, are doing fine. The other day I sent three emissaries, aged seven to ten, to call on the bears at the Rock Creek Park zoo. They report the ex-cubs are grown now, and in stalwart condition, with a sign over their premises stating they are the gift of the President of Korea to the President of the United States of America. Harvey Firestone's pygmy hippos from Liberia are likewise thriving. . . .

To my regret several pieces are not included. They haven't

been rejected by the Official Committee on Unofficial Publications—at least, not yet. They haven't been written. There is, for instance, the story of how Andrei Vishinsky, the Soviet Foreign Minister, failed to get from Paris to Warsaw in the private car supplied by the Wagons-Lit Company. Vishinsky rode in it in style as far as the Bavaria-Czech frontier but near Cheb he was dumped out in the snow against the free side of the winter Iron Curtain, with no galoshes and a seething bad temper. When, hours later, he clattered into Prague, bouncing on the wooden benches of a third-class coach of the nationalized Czechoslovak Railway, Vishinsky was the angry man, and the satellite officials who were gathered in shivering conclave to receive him on the platform had a rough going over. Members of the Soviet Embassy in Prague received more abrasive treatment still, to the edification of their American colleagues, whose contribution to events goes as yet unrecorded. Sometime when I'm low in spirit I'll cheer myself up by setting forth the details of that incident and its sequel.

Then there is the tale of the Japanese game warden who discovered martinis. We were hunting mallards and geese near Hokkaido and spent the night in a paper-walled inn drenched by frozen spray from the northwest Pacific. The warden mistook our martinis, lovingly blended the day before by Peggy Parsons in our embassy in Tokyo and poured back into bottles, for a superior brand of tea-house American saki. His experience was educational. The next day we kept a shotgun away from the warden as long as we could, thereafter permitting him to shoot only at cripples.

Finally, I had hoped to include a piece on woodcock shooting in my own state of Maine, just to get the Foreign Service world back into focus. For a man who likes to carry a twenty-gauge double there isn't anything anywhere that compares with October New England, with alder swamps bordered by gray birch and, higher up, thickets of young white pine and hemlocks. A frost the night before, and at the edge of the field the late blueberries are sugar-sweet underfoot. The white setter is working upwind. The flaming leaves still cling to their criss-crossed branches. A woodcock corkscrewing out of the alders is the fastest shot in the world—the most satisfying of all targets.

The way things have been, I get back to Maine only one October in three. That's the only complaint I have against life in the Foreign Service.

Georgetown, D.C., July 1956

P.S.

And now Brazil, a vast improbable land full of hospitality and great distances—a land big as the United States plus an extra Texas. Over in Mato Grosso, seven hours from Rio by air, they tell of a *fazenda* twice as big as the King Ranch, where the land slopes toward the Gran Chaco and the echo of shotgun shooting startles only the *jacú* and the *capivara*. And off the bulge of the continent, two hundred miles into the ocean, lies Fernando de Noronha, nesting ground of the Snark—and other diverting hallucinations.

There should, I hope, be more tales to tell in the future.

Rio de Janeiro, February 1957

The Biggest Frog in the World

AT CALLAO, in Peru, I was once a vice consul. I was full of ambition, illusions, and the conviction—convenient to the taxpayers who employed me—that no matter how improbable the project something, somehow, ought to be done about it. A letter had arrived from the United States and from it I shook a crumpled ten-dollar bill. The letter read:

Mr. Consul

I grow the frog for market in New Orleans and on dit [crossed out] they tell of biggest the frog he comes from Peru. Please to send me one dozen those biggest of frogs, six the masculine and six the female. There is no trouble. Masculine has larger the ears—like fifty-cent piece.

I send ten dollars with thanks and respectfully, Mr. Consul.

Alfonse Boucher

The return address was in Louisiana, and I pictured my correspondent prowling web-footedly through his marshes, but full of zeal and desirous of improving his breeding stock by crossing his bayou bullfrogs with their Peruvian cousins. A dark little man, I pictured, paying his way in the world. It was probably as fair a picture as we have of Alfonse.

Here was something more satisfying than certifying health papers for R.M.S. *Oropesa*—Valparaiso to Liverpool via the Panama Canal—or replying to Herbert Hoover's Commerce Department questionnaires about the market for brassieres and roller skates in Arequipa. Here was something that made sense about being a vice consul.

I took out my Appleton's Spanish-English dictionary to look up "frog"; then I summoned Carlos, my Peruvian clerk. "Carlos," I said, "dice una carta que en el Peru se encuentra la rana mas grande del mundo. ¿Es verdad?"

"Si, señor," said Carlos. "En la montaña hay muchas ranas." Which was to say: In the montaña there are many frogs.

The montaña is eastern Peru, a piece of real estate somewhat larger than Texas and ten times as wet. It is the land of the Amazon tributaries—the Ucayali, the Marañon, the Mantaro, the Urubamba—and scores of other great muddy rivers, each as wide as the Hudson River opposite Yonkers. Carlos' reply did not perceptibly narrow the scope of inquiry.

"You said 'many frogs,'" I told Carlos. "But are they *big* frogs?"

"Si, señor," repeated Carlos. "En la montaña hay muchas ranas, bastante grandes." In the montaña there are many big frogs.

Maybe I should have known better than to take on Alfonse's enterprise but "Masculine has larger the ears—like fifty-cent piece" was catnip to a growing vice consul. My consul general in Lima, a man filled with daily apprehension lest the State Department should, as he put it, come back at him, took a pessimistic view of my prospects.

"You will," the consul general predicted, "waste a lot of time chasing a lot of goddam Andean bullfrogs. What's more, you can't ship a crate of live frogs to New Orleans for only ten dollars. It'll be just like Dr. Noguchi's monkeys."

My chief referred to an incident painful to him, of recent occurrence. Noguchi was a Japanese doctor, and his monkeys were sent to Peru for experiments in connection with *verrugas,* a wart disease then afflicting the upper valleys. Since the Rockefeller Foundation was sponsoring Dr. Noguchi, his monkeys reached Callao in care of the American consul, and after one of the cages slipped its sling and broke open on the Callao pier, I spent an active weekend chasing recalcitrant Liberian *monos* all over Peru's principal seaport—up and down the masts of Grace ships and as far afield as Maggie Blanco's Rimac bordello. On Maggie's adobe roof we ran the last three chattering monkeys to shelter. I effected their capture with the assistance of small boys hired for the purpose—fishermen's sons who, while the American vice consul pacified the monkeys with bananas, threw over their heads the net called *teralla,* which spins out in a circle like a lasso and comes down symmetrically with lead weights around the edge.

My banana-*teralla* technique astonished the Liberian monkeys, and it also astonished Maggie's Sunday patrons, but the consul general, when faced with the bill for recapturing Dr. Noguchi's pets, had not been gratified.

"So if you want to chase bullfrogs," my chief warned me, "do it on your own time. The consulate general has no funds to finance a trip to Amazonia." He was a man much chastened by the Consular Regulations, which he quoted freely for the instruction of fledgling vice consuls.

Somewhat abashed by lack of support from the consul general, I wrote an interim reply to Louisiana. I acknowledged the receipt of Alfonse's ten dollars. I said preliminary inquiry—meaning Carlos, my consular clerk—had failed to establish the facts but that my investigation would continue. On one point however I felt it fair to warn Alfonse. Not being an expert on frogs I doubted whether I could tell the sex of one frog from another. If I discovered those biggest of frogs, I wrote, Alfonse would have to accept them higgledy-piggledy, one sex or another; gender was the consignee's responsibility.

The office of W. R. Grace and Company, around the corner from my upstairs vice consulate in Callao, confirmed the fact that their freighters served New Orleans from the Rainless Coast. The Callao manager, when I showed him Alfonse's letter, was affable. He said he could probably find a skipper to carry my crate of frogs from Peru to New Orleans as personal baggage, without bill of lading, and I could keep Alfonse's ten dollars to hunt frogs with—if I found any.

Encouraged by the public-spirited attitude of the Casa Grace, I took the trolley to Lima, seven miles through dusty fields of cotton, and I headed for the Museo Arqueologico.

Sure enough, in the pottery reproductions of Peru during the Pachacamac civilization there were *huacos* of llamas and alpacas and of dogs and fish, and of frogs large enough to scare the pants off an Oklahoma jack rabbit. Baked clay vessels in the shape of frogs, dating back centuries to the time of the Great Chimu: *huacos* in pink and brown and green, skillfully wrought, that showed the frogs of Peru as muscular citizens, with ears as big as Inca subway tokens.

The caretaker of the museum, wearing black-button shoes and much in need of a shave, volunteered information. "*Si, señor,*" he said, "*en la sierra hay muchas ranas.*" In the sierra, there are many frogs. Certainly, he said, some of them would be large frogs. Very large, and he made expansive gestures. But where in the sierra? Ah, señor, the sierra is a wide place. No doubt on the other side of the cordillera. And would the señor be interested in seeing the pornographic *huacos:* very diverting, available for a small additional fee—no photographs to be taken.

I thanked him and said another time, and I emerged from the museum into the winter mist of Lima, feeling that progress had been achieved. If there were frogs in Peru in pre-Inca times, there ought to be frogs in Peru today, and, unless the modelers in ancient clay were bent on deceiving future generations, the Peruvian frogs were of noble dimensions.

Inquiries over the next several days having produced negative results—and the time taken for those inquiries having perhaps been to the detriment of the transaction of the taxpayers' regular consular business—I concluded that Alfonse's problem deserved publicity. Accordingly, in my Callao vice consulate I drafted a letter to the newspapers, which Carlos with much diligence translated into Spanish for the Lima press. In it I described Alfonse's predicament, deleting his observations on sex, and I quoted the following paragraph which I found in the *Encyclopaedia Britannica:*

> Some frogs [wrote the frog savant of the encyclopaedia]
> grow to a large size. The bullfrog of eastern United States
> and Canada, reaching a length of nearly eight inches from
> snout to vent, long regarded as the giant of the genus, has
> been surpassed by the discovery of *Rana guppyi* (eight and
> one-half inches) in the Solomon Islands, and of *Rana goliath*
> (ten inches) in the South Cameroons. . . .

Here was an opportunity, my letter to the press declared,
which should appeal to the patriotism of every Peruvian.
Here was a chance to prove to the world that in Peru with
its diversity of natural resources there existed a frog of impressive, of truly epic proportions. A frog such as the pre-
Inca pottery makers had rendered imperishable in their
huacos. A frog that would make *Rana goliath* look like a
tadpole.

I was uplifted by my own eloquence, and apparently so
was Carlos, because he warmed up my text with some
hortatory phrases of his own. I signed my name to the Spanish translation, adding my official title: *Vice consul de los
Estados Unidos de Norteamerica.* I sat back to await developments, which were not long in coming.

The springs of patriotism pour lava-hot among the Good
Neighbors, and Peru is no exception. The publication of my
frog letter not only inundated my modest vice consulate in
Callao, but swamped the consulate general in Lima as well.
It flooded the American embassy, which was busy trying to
negotiate a settlement of the Tacna Arica problem. Stimulated by my challenge to national pride, for days our correspondence burgeoned.

A professor at San Marcos University suggested the upper Huallaga River, somewhere, he recalled, between
Yurimaguas and Tingo María. My atlas identified the towns
but they were two hundred miles apart and each was several

days from railhead by horseback and canoe. A vanadium miner referred me to a stream that flows past Cajamarca, where Pizarro slew the last of the Incas. It would have taken me a week to get there. An *hacendado* from Chiclayo remembered a frog in an irrigation canal west of Olmos. That too was far from Lima. Some of the replies enclosed maps, but none of the places mentioned were within walking distance of the capital. There were also phone calls. And when our Lima volunteers subsided, *El Comercio* and *La Prensa* had penetrated to the provinces and there was a second deluge of correspondence, this time accompanied by sample frogs, some of which after postal exposure were no longer in the pink of batrachian condition.

Most of the replies—and most of the dead frogs—were delivered to the Lima consulate general. I was summoned from Callao to hear what the consul general thought of my activities, in words that would have alerted the stevedores of Hoboken.

"Furthermore," concluded my harrassed chief, "since when do vice consuls sign letters to the newspapers? Any letters leaving this office hereafter go out over my signature." And he told me to take out the dead frogs and bury them, which I did, but not until I had ascertained that according to the formula established by the *Encyclopaedia Britannica,* none of my trophies measured as much as ten inches. They were formidable frogs and they had discs for ears, about the size of quarters, but even alive they haven't been championship *ranas.*

Meanwhile my dossier on frogs, including letters addressed to the embassy which were forwarded to me with a rubber-stamp notation "Respectfully referred to the Consulate for acknowledgement and action," was bursting out of my single cabinet in Callao and covering Carlos' typewriter table. The file now included a penciled expression of thanks-in-anticipation from Alfonse in his Louisiana bayou; he reiterated that sex would prove no obstacle because "masculine has larger the ears." But none of my frogs was as large as *rana guppyi* from the Solomon Islands, and thus far Peru was clearly outclassed by *rana goliath,* the giant frog from the Cameroons. I was beginning to wish I had stuck to my crew lists and bills of health, my consular invoices, and my markets for brassieres and roller skates in Arequipa.

It was the American ambassador who came to my rescue. A former senator and an impressive gentleman, the ambassador to Peru was no chair-warming diplomat but a traveler of distinction who conceived it his job to move around the country, learning what made it tick. He had been away when my frog letter hit the Lima newsstands, but he had it before him when I called at his office, by request, and in some trepidation.

"From what the consul general tells me," declared my ambassador, "your letter lighted a bonfire. We haven't had so much correspondence since last time Congress raised the tariff on Peruvian cotton. Even President Leguia is interested. This morning when I finished talking to him about the Arica plebiscite, he wanted to know how our frog campaign was going. Said he himself remembered seeing a giant frog in the Urubamba River. How about it?"

"We have news of a lot of frogs," I reported, "and some sent in have been pretty big, but they aren't world's record. I'm getting sort of discouraged about the whole project, Mr. Ambassador."

"I'll say we've got a lot of frogs," mused the ambassador. "They shout *ancas de rana*—that's frog legs—every time my wife goes to the market. Here at the office the boys complain they can't code telegrams because of interruptions from people who want to tell us about frogs. Where do we go from here?"

"I've plenty of leads," I replied. "Some of them sound promising. But they're all outside Lima and most of them are over the cordillera. Fact is, sir, it takes most of my time acknowledging the letters."

The ambassador considered the problem. "Tell you what I'll do," he said presently. "You pick out a batch of the likeliest letters and send them around to me. I've poked into a lot of corners of Peru. Mark the envelope 'personal.' Maybe we can figure out something."

He shook hands, and when I went out I heard him chuckling. At the door of the embassy I bumped into an Indian woman with straw hat and pigtails who tried to sell me frogs out of a basket. In Maine they would have been pretty good bullfrogs, but they weren't up to Alfonse's requirements.

Three days later I was back in the ambassadorial presence. "This letter from the Canadian padre near Huancayo," said the ambassador. "He says the biggest frogs he's ever seen are in the Mantaro River. Whoppers. I know Father Pierre and he's a stout citizen. And since he comes from Quebec he ought to know his bullfrogs."

I said, diffidently, that I remembered the padre's letter.

"I've been wanting," continued the ambassador, "to get up to Lake Junín for a long time, for the duck hunting. The Cerro de Pasco people have a hut near the lake, which is the source of the Mantaro River Father Pierre writes about. Maybe we can combine frogs with ducks. I'll get off a note to the padre."

When I mentioned the consul general, the ambassador dismissed that official. "I've already spoken to him. I said I needed an assistant. Lugging ammunition at fourteen thousand feet is no work for an oldster, and besides—I hear you shoot."

As for the frogs, the ambassador suggested I take Alfonse's ten dollars and buy several stout nets, like butterfly nets but of heavier material, with an iron ring about two feet across and plenty of depth to each net. "Attach the rings to bamboo poles eight or ten feet long. And you better have a crate made," concluded the ambassador.

I said, "Yes, sir." And within the hour Carlos and I were busily shopping.

We left Lima in style, in the private Pullman car *Atahualpa*, loaned to the ambassador by the manager of the Central Railroad of Peru, which is the highest railway in the world. That afternoon we crossed the continental divide at sixteen thousand feet, with snowdrifts on either side of the track. In the rarefied air the engine coughed and strained, and the smoke shredded away from the funnel. Around us, looking as though they had nothing much to do, stood Indians with barrel chests, wearing ponchos and red knitted caps with earflaps. A man develops a set of lungs at that altitude.

Below the pass, and to the north and south, stretched the great Andean *altiplano* of Peru, where the Indian population lives on barley and wheat and on the products of the mines worked for centuries by the Spanish conquerors, and before that for centuries by the Incas. At Oroya, beside the Cerro de Pasco smelter, the Canadian padre came aboard —a man as big as the ambassador, with a beard and a twinkling eye. The train turned north along the Mantaro River which, five thousand miles from the Atlantic Ocean, looked like a promising trout stream. It also looked as though it might have bullfrogs in it, and on the subject of frogs the padre was optimistic.

"First the ducks," responded the ambassador.

At nightfall the *Atahualpa* deposited us near the shore of Lake Junín, crimson in the sunset blazing over the western cordillera. There were tall reeds around the lake, and as the train skirted the shore I saw hundreds of coots go tearing across the water. The tropical night closed down, cold on the roof of the world, under an infinity of stars.

Our sod hut was chinked with mud against the wind. We

ate roast mutton and *papas huancayinas,* while two Indian boys stoked the fire. After supper Father Pierre lighted one of the ambassador's cigars, thriftily placing it on the window sill while he performed his evening devotions, but the ambassador said he needed all the oxygen he could get at that altitude, undiluted.

Of our hunting the next day I can remember that walking across the frozen grass from the hut to the lake, weighted with two shotguns and our ammunition, took as much breath as a five-mile run at sea level. We poled through the reeds in balsa boats as the first light stained the eastern cordillera. And when the sun rose behind the peaks, leaving the blue lake in shadow, a great flock of flamingos flew over us. We were in shade and the birds, high up, hundreds of them, were as pink in the sunlight as strawberry ice-cream sodas.

We shot over two hundred ducks, most of which on our return the ambassador gave to hospitals in Lima. I remember that shooting at fourteen thousand feet required a recal-

culation of lead and trajectory, and that the kick was formidable. We also shot a fine batch of coots for the Indian guides,
our helpers counting the birds two-by-two, after the Quichua
practice, instead of one-two-three-four, as we do.

We spent a second night in the hut, with Father Pierre
doing things over eucalyptus coals with the teal. We washed
down the ducks with red wine from the Ica Valley.

"And now," said Father Pierre, happily inhaling a fresh
cigar, "about these Andean bullfrogs."

It was too cold, said Father Pierre, to find our frogs around
the lake or in the immediate reaches of the Mantaro River.
Thing to do was to get back aboard the *Atahualpa*, which was
returning for us the following morning, and ride down the
line, well below Oroya. "Frogs live around here," he said,
"but they're mostly small ones. You have to get down to where
eucalyptus will grow—around ten or eleven thousand feet.
There the river is wider and slower, with grass and reeds and
water hyacinths. The railroad parallels the river all the way
to Huancayo, with sidings every few kilometers where we can
stop the train and go frogging."

And that was the way we did it.

For ten dollars Alfonse in his Louisiana bayou had a private
train in Peru consisting of the Pullman car *Atahualpa*, a
caboose for the crew, and a locomotive and tender. For
hunters, Alfonse had one American ambassador, one American vice consul, and Father Pierre (who remarked that this
was fair enough, since if Alfonse's forebears had remained
in Acadie, Alfonse might have been one of Father Pierre's
parishioners). For assistant hunters, Alfonse had the train
crew, including two interested locomotive engineers and the
brakeman, plus uncounted Indians who left off their harvesting and flocked to the river bank in droves, wherever we
stopped. This interfered with our operations, and the padre
admonished the Indians in Quichua, whereat the line of
spectators would obediently sway back a few yards from

the edge of the Mantaro River only to surge forward again, augmented, as newcomers pressed ahead to see what manner of river-bank negotiations were afoot.

The nets worked admirably as we toiled and sweated in the Andean sunshine. The frogs, as the padre had written, were whoppers. Some we found in the weeds and grass near the shore. Others lurked on the bank. When startled they curved upward in long leaping parabolas, each striking the river with the *plunk* of a stove lid. They were wonderful frogs and not easy to catch, but never was exercise more richly rewarded. One by one the records of New England, of the Solomon Islands, and finally of the African Cameroons collapsed under the blue sky of the Peruvian sierra.

Appropriately it was Father Pierre who netted the champion specimen, the frog that vanquished *Rana goliath* of the *Encyclopaedia Britannica*, although our padre fell into the Mantaro River—habit and all, including his round black hat—in making the capture. That halted the hunt and we repaired to the *Atahualpa* for dry clothes and a fresh cigar for our guide, while I measured our trophies.

We had twenty-eight frogs, more than enough for Alfonse and his frog farm. The body of the new champion was eleven inches long—again by encyclopaedia computation: not counting the length of his plump tapering legs. Father Pierre christened him Reginald; when stretched out on a moist board, which Reginald didn't like, he measured almost two feet overall, to the tips of his twitching toes. When we deposited him in his box Reginald sat up, looking belligerent, and his ears—those flat disks on either side of his head—were enough like fifty-cent pieces to have rung a cash register.

We returned to Lima in triumph, and shortly thereafter the ambassador invited the captain of a Grace Line freighter to the embassy residence for cocktails, over which we gave him advice on the care and feeding of bullfrogs. Insects, we advised, were staple diet for traveling batrachians. Before leaving the sierra we had collected several bushels of assorted gnats, *comejenes*, moths, *polillas*, mosquitoes, ants, and beetles by the device of hanging an electric lantern outside Father Pierre's chapel in Huancayo, and then sweeping up the survivors.

Reginald, on his departure for the ship, looked almost genial.

The rest of my tale is depressing, for Alfonse on his bayou never received his bullfrogs. That spring the Mississippi River burst through its levees. In Lima we read of floods all down the lower valley. New Orleans was safe, but disaster stalked the delta area. The bayous were inundated.

When the Grace Line freighter *Santa Rita* returned to Callao six weeks after I had seen Reginald and his brethren aboard, I paused only for the yellow quarantine flag before rallying to the captain's cabin. I found that worthy mariner in his undershirt, waiting to complete the port formalities before turning in after a night in the Pacific fog off San Lorenzo Island.

"I got the frogs to New Orleans all right," said the Captain. "We almost ran out of grub. That biggest frog ate cockroaches the last week of the trip—and loved 'em! Five frogs died but we got the rest of them to the pier in good shape. But we couldn't deliver the consignment."

"The floods?"

"That's right. The floods. Washed those poor frog-catching Cajuns clear into the Gulf of Mexico. Hell of a flood. Son, the Mississippi River is angry water. All the company in New Orleans could find out was that your consignee, in that parish you gave me the name of, was missing. After all the trouble the ambassador went to, I was downright disappointed about it. It was tough luck, but there it was. No Alfonse. And me with twenty-three damn bullfrogs, which the customs was suspicious of anyway, there being no bill of lading."

I didn't feel cheerful, there in the skipper's cabin aft of the bridge of the *Santa Rita*. "What did you do then?" I asked the captain.

"Ha!" said the skipper. "Weren't enough cockroaches aboard to feed the frogs back to Callao. Told the customs so. Told the company the shipment was their responsibility. There's a zoo in New Orleans, and that's what we did with them. Sixteen of them, that is. We got a frog expert from the zoo. He picked out eight males and eight females. Said the males have larger ears."

I did arithmetic. Twenty-eight frogs left Callao. Five died en route. Sixteen went to the New Orleans zoo. That left seven frogs unaccounted for. I pointed out this discrepancy to the skipper, who favored me with an articulate nautical wink, captain to vice consul. "That's right," said the skipper. "It left me seven frogs. I took them to Antoine's Restaurant. And boy—did they do a job on those frogs' legs! But your giant frog, the one you and the ambassador were so proud of—he went to the zoo. I reckon he's busy there, propagating the species. . . ."

Those adventures happened many years ago. Ambassador Poindexter and the good Father Pierre are long since called to their rewards, which I hope are great. Today, when I go out hunting, I often take along a vice consul to help carry the ammunition.

It was not until after the war that I visited New Orleans. I was sailing for a new post in South America and I received generous attention from the city officials who take pride in the relations between that great Louisiana port and the countries of Latin America.

In New Orleans the mayor took me to a famous restaurant and outside I paused to admire the assortment of seafood assembled to impress the beholder. It greatly impressed the beholder. There were clawless lobsters and pink shrimps from Yucatán, and dark-shelled Moro crabs from Batabanó in Cuba. There were pompano and pargo, clear-eyed from the Gulf of Mexico. Dangling jointed legs and an upholstered chassis proclaimed the *centolla,* brought all the way from the Strait of Magellan. There were *haibas blandas* from Antofagasta, and conger eels from Valparaiso.

And in the center of this rich display, crouching on a bed of watercress and wearing an arrogant expression, was the largest frog since the *Encyclopaedia Britannica* went into its thirtieth edition. *Rana super goliath,* read the notice in the restaurant window: *Giant Frog From Peru.*

It was Reginald's great-great-grandson. And his ears were as big as fifty-cent pieces.

Snakes, Pepper Birds, and Wild Guineas in Liberia

THE FIRST man to be appointed "Special Representative of the President of the United States with the Personal Rank of Ambassador"—a title that during World War II was to become as exclusive as the right to ride on the New York subway—was Major General Blanton Winship, who in 1933 was sent to Liberia. Winship, a fine soldier and a superlative wing shot, was a personal friend of outgoing Secretary of State Henry L. Stimson, who asked him if he would go to Liberia under an official mandate of the new administration. President-Elect Roosevelt approved Winship's appointment, and in an afterthought of geniality invented the title "with the Personal Rank of Ambassador."

Winship was judge advocate general of the Army at the time and dubious about buying Liberian adventures without peeking under the mosquito netting. But when Roosevelt mentioned the governorship of Puerto Rico as a possibility *after* Liberia, Winship said he would go, provided Secretary Stimson would find him a young man who, as the general put it, "knew something about the Liberian background." In those days my own official card read "Third Secretary of Legation of the United States of America," and because the last American representative had died of yellow fever, candidates for the Winship expedition were not exactly cluttering up Pennsylvania Avenue at 17th Street in front of the old State War Navy Building. It was in those somewhat meager circumstances that I was elected to accompany General Winship to Liberia.

The general and I had in the Firestones from Akron. The Firestone Tire and Rubber Company had recently leased one million Liberian acres to grow rubber on, and presently someone said something about bird shooting. Winship and I forthwith bought a pair of knockabout shotguns and felt better about the assignment.

In London we had our inoculations for yellow fever. Noguchi had recently completed his experiments with monkeys, with results favorable to Noguchi, and the general and I were Numbers 51 and 52 at the hospital of the Institute of Tropical Studies. The inoculation was given with a hypodermic needle the size of a Flit gun, and the medico in charge predicted a headache the next day, which turned out to be the understatement of all experience. The S.S.

Wahehe—six thousand tons, Hamburg and Southampton for Las Palmas, Dakar, Sierra Leone, and the Bight of Benim—bobbed like a cork on the Bay of Biscay, while General Winship and I edged south with a roaring fever.

Mamba Point, named for the African cobras thereon, showed dimly through the gray rain off the *Wahehe* port side two weeks from Southampton, and we came ashore in rowboats through the surf at Monrovia, using our raincoats to wrap up our shotguns.

Liberia had a president, with whom we transacted frequent official business. It had a constitution patterned after our own. It had a secretary of state whose diplomatic notes bristled with *ipso facto, locum tenens, au courant,* and some of the longest English words to be found in Webster's unabridged dictionary. It also had a jail, close by the American legation. The jail was full of prisoners with time on their hands. When the general shook the legation bell to summon a whisky and soda, the prisoners in unison shouted "Boy!" to the indignation of the legation staff, who objected to being ordered around by jailbirds.

There were six thousand people in Monrovia, and one horse. Grass grew in the principal streets and from time to time the prisoners were brought out under guard and set to weeding Broadway, which they cleared in dispirited fashion while transacting business with unincarcerated supporters who squatted among the weeds and made passes at the mosquitoes. We had two worthless cats in the legation named Aedes and Anopheles, after the mosquitoes. We also had flying cockroaches, big as tri-motor Fords and twice as shiny. Now and then a houseboy would bat one down and then bite it. "Bugabug, you chop'm fine," the houseboy would declare—meaning: delicious.

A ship called every twenty-eight days at Monrovia with mail and supplies. The supplies mildewed overnight—along with our shoes and our official correspondence; and if the fresh food wasn't consumed at once by the cockroaches, it had usually spoiled anyway by the next morning. The notion of game, and especially of game birds, shortly became an obsession. We started inquiring of Liberian officials.

A geyser of misinformation followed. Elephants, we were told, stomped around practically at will, just outside the capital. They kept pulling down the newly installed telephone wires connecting Monrovia with the Firestone plantation. The government would be happy to have us chase an elephant—better still, several elephants. We asked, What Else Had They? and were told—Bushcows. Those, so we subsequently discovered, are related to the carrabao of the Philippines—mean citizens with ugly horns, ticks on their tummies, and no sense of humor: fine targets for a Holland and Holland Magnum but relatively immune to birdshot. We thanked our hosts again, and we asked, What Else Is There? We were told there were crocodiles thirteen feet long in the Mensurado River, and larger ones down the coast near Junktown. Inland from Monrovia, various optimistic local Chiefs guaranteed that they would find us a hippopotamus "just like the one Harvey Firestone gave to President Coolidge."

Bird shooting? Oh, yes, said our obliging informants, there was bird shooting too—wild guinea fowl; likewise peacocks; any number of wild pigeons. Fine bird shooting, close to Monrovia. And as an afterthought they added: If you don't mind the snakes.

Snakes, we discovered, were only one of several factors complicating our bird shooting. Other factors included the Time Element (which simultaneously involved the Snake Problem), the African Wage Scale (whereby the Palm Tree shilling threatened to undo us), and the Enthusiasm of our Diplomatic Colleagues, who knew nothing whatever about bird shooting but looked forward to eating the game they hoped we'd bring back—provided we outwitted the snakes, dominated the time element, and liquidated the wage scale. "Wild guineas," said the diplomats, "you chop'm fine"— meaning: very tasty.

Snakes, nevertheless, became our number one priority. Without fetching out an atlas and offering to take on professional herpetologists, I estimate that the year round there are more snakes per acre in coastal Liberia than there are blackflies in a Maine cedar swamp the first week of June. There are all kinds of snakes in Liberia, and many of them have fangs full of poison. The unpoisonous Liberian snakes are the pythons, and Syrian traders along the Monrovia water front quickly discovered that pythons make better rat-catchers than tomcats do. A brisk market in juvenile pythons developed around this discovery, so that when I ventured into the establishment of Ibrahim Khouy in search of mosquito netting for the legation a few mornings after my arrival, there was seven feet of python contentedly lapping condensed milk at the far end of the counter. When it came to measuring my purchase, the python came eagerly down the counter, apparently offering his two meters' worth as a part of the bargain. Ibrahim nonchalantly wiped condensed milk off the python's chin with a silk pocket handkerchief while he figured my account with the other hand. That would be seventeen shillings, and what else could his humble emporium offer? From the doorway I told Ibrahim to charge it, and to send the package—minus python—to the American Legation. The python slithered back to his saucer of condensed milk but Ibrahim followed me to the legation automobile. "Python too big," he explained, with a gesture of passing a razor from one furry ear to the other, "then you chop'm fine"—meaning: python chowder.

The poisonous Liberian snakes, which abounded in the grassy plains likewise inhabited by wild guineas, included the vipers and the mambas. Vipers are true cousins to the rattlesnakes of Texas—sluggish serpents as long and thick

as your arm, and it takes their poison about an hour to produce coronary thrombosis. But the real terror of Liberia is
the mamba—the black mamba and the green mamba. A
mamba strikes like a whiplash and can travel across open
ground as fast as a startled bird hunter, minus his shotgun,
can gallop. Mambas belong to the cobra clan, and they take
an unfriendly view of intruders. Mamba Point, just south
of Monrovia, was alive with them. When we built a new
legation on Mamba Point a few years after General Winship's assignment, we had to pay time and a half to local
artisans to persuade them even to visit the property. On the
same site, we eventually erected the first snakeproof legation on record.

To meet the snake problem, the general and I devised two elements of protection. From a local doctor serving the Health Section of the League of Nations we obtained flat tins put up by the firm of Pasteur of Paris. One was green and one was red, and each contained a hypodermic syringe and a phial of serum derived from uneager members of the snake community in São Paulo, south of Rio de Janeiro. It was the idea that if a viper bit you, you used the green serum, and lived happily ever after. The red was for mamba, and Dr. Mackenzie said it took a fast man with a needle to beat the paralysis of mamba venom. As an afterthought, the doctor observed that it wasn't always easy, under field conditions, to determine which snake had bit you!

Our second safeguard was more prosaic. By persistent use of the Firestone communications service we obtained two pairs of leggings, designed by Raymond Ditmars, who was curator of reptiles at the New York Zoological Park. Ditmars had more than a passing acquaintance with the snakes of West Africa. His contraption was shaped like a hussar's boot, high in the knee, minus the foot, and ended in a strap to go under the instep. The material was light, tightly woven canvas, two layers, with a layer of fine copper mesh in between. The wire was so fine that snake fangs were supposed to stop there, frustrated and blunted. General Winship and I tried it with a needle, and sure enough, the point was stopped by the copper netting. This was encouraging, even though the wire had a tendency to wrinkle at the bottom and gouge our ankles. But as Dr. Ditmars declared, eighty per cent of snakebites occur below the knee, where his leggings gave us ample protection.

The Time Element was even more complicated. Six degrees from the equator it gets dark when the sun goes down, as if a black curtain were suddenly lowered over the western horizon. Because of business with Liberian officials in the mornings, we could hunt only in the afternoons and it was important to return to the road—the one road that led back to Monrovia from the hinterland—before darkness engulfed the land and snakes became invisible to game-laden hunters. Our almanac indicated the sun set in those latitudes at six-seven p.m. and it was pitch dark ten minutes later. Hence our interest in accurate timing.

There wasn't any radio time service in Liberia then, and the noon gun fired every day proved a most unreliable indicator. Our watches, so we had thought, were fairly accurate. But each day when we set our watches by the noon gun in Monrovia, we had to move them twenty minutes ahead, or else retard them by half an hour. Translated into sunset terms and the prospect of meeting a mamba out for an evening stroll, this was a serious problem.

Investigation revealed that every morning, about half an hour before the noon gun was fired, a small boy would emerge from the Presidency and head for the hilltop. He was naked, except for a single adornment—a large metal alarm clock suspended from his little finger. Sometimes he balanced the alarm clock on the top of his head, but mostly he carried it, according to orders, suspended from his little finger. Clearly he was on his way to tell the soldier of the Liberian Frontier Force, who would presently fire the noon gun, what the official time was in Liberia. That much was understandable but the question remained, Who set the alarm clock? We were told that the president set the alarm clock. So far, so good; but what did the president of the republic do about setting the presidential watch that he used to set the presidential alarm clock with?

This involved us in further research but we were finally informed—apparently on competent authority—that the president set his watch every morning by the pepper bird.

The pepper bird is a lively character of moderately regular habits, including a penchant for early morning disturbance. Most of the Monrovia gardens have pepper birds which are the traditional West African equivalent of the cock-that-crows-with-the-dawning. More than once the general and I had been brought upright beneath our mosquito nettings by the pepper bird, and it didn't take long for us to decide we could do without him.

But the pepper bird was hardly a metronome geared to modern civilization, and we took an astigmatic view of possibly being stranded after sunset in high grass because the presidential pepper bird had been out late the night before with a hornbill.

Word of our research was presently carried to the president. The president was indignant. He declared, through an emissary, that it was a canard. A century before, perhaps, it might have happened when Liberia was being colonized by illiterate ex-slaves, and the Paramount Chiefs hadn't learned the difference between two-timing each other and two-timing the Firestones, but not in modern Liberia. No president, we were assured, had set his watch by the pepper bird since Grand Bassa was formally admitted to the Liberian Union.

But how then, we persisted—secure in our diplomatic immunity—did the president of the republic set the watch that he used to set the alarm clock that the small boy carried to the top of the hill to set the clock the soldier of the Liberian Frontier Force used when he fired the noon gun over Monrovia? Just how was *that* watch set? Who set the official time for Liberia?

We were told, and not in a tone that encouraged further argument, that in twentieth-century Liberia the president set his watch by the noon gun, the same as the rest of the citizens. . . .

The Palm Tree shilling became our first practical lesson in Liberian economy. The Liberian budget was voted in Liberian dollars, but there weren't any dollars, Liberian or American, in Liberia. The circulating medium was the Palm

Tree shilling from Sierra Leone, the Gold Coast, and Nigeria. It was at par with the British shilling, and one shilling represented a day's wage for an able-bodied Liberian. We overlooked this fact the first time we went hunting. We drove out the main road past the palms with birds' nests swinging in gray hammocks from the fronds, past patches of "high bush" which was impenetrable rain-drenched equatorial forest, and came fifteen miles inland to open savanna-knee-high grass that looked like excellent cover for game birds. The grass stretched for miles in every direction, and there were patches of cassava and sweet potato, scummy pools of green water, and rice fields that attracted hundreds and hundreds of pigeons that roosted in the high bush but came down each evening to drink and to peck at the rice grains.

We decided we needed assistants to carry the birds we hoped to shoot, and to beat the grass to flush out the wild guineas. Manpower, it immediately appeared, was no difficult problem. Although the land seemed sparsely populated our legation automobile was soon surrounded by interested youngsters, eager to take part in whatever proceedings impended. We recruited half a dozen in no time, and set forth gingerly across the nearest savanna, alert for vipers and mambas. That first afternoon convinced us the land was alive with game birds, and, considering our pre-occupation with snakes, we fared not too badly.

At sunset we were back beside the car, and I doled out six Palm Tree shillings, one to each astonished helper. A clamor arose but as it didn't sound disappointed or indignant we gave it no mind and drove back to the capital through the gelatinous darkness. That night the beat of drums rolled down the Mensurado River, but we gave that no mind either.

The explanation came when we returned up country two days later. The previously deserted savanna was alive with Liberian citizens, some of whom hailed from as far away as the Firestone plantation. And every citizen was a candidate for chasing wild guineas with the American hunters. We were mobbed by gesticulating candidates, congregated in hundreds. Their rallying cry was, "One shilling, mister." The savanna was a shambles and the nearest game bird had stopped five miles away, without looking over his shoulder. It took us a week to reorganize our expeditions, and even on a sixpence-for-three-hours basis, we had to recruit a foreman to select ten boys each afternoon, and to restrain scores of disappointed applicants. The Firestone manager, thirty miles away, felt the repercussions of our enterprise long after our departure from Liberia.

The shooting, after we learned to move through the grass and became accustomed to the warm drenching rain that sluiced off the sweat and then dried in the scorching sun-light, was wonderful. The guineas made the same potracking noise they make in the United States and the Caribbean, but there the resemblance ended. The Liberian guinea is a brown bird the size of a New England ruffed grouse. It is a fast-moving target, handicapped by the absence of bushes

but smart enough to run on the ground and flush far ahead of the hunter. We moved abreast about a gunshot apart, with boys between us and the rest of them fanning out on either side. When they got the idea, they made excellent beaters, barring only the temptation to go charging ahead whenever a bird broke cover. They were incredible about snakes, sensing their proximity with an instinct altogether denied us. Most of the boys were stark naked, with now and then the flash of a pink sole-of-foot when its owner jumped over a dangerously moving grass patch. None of the boys was bitten. As for the hunters, General Winship and I continued to wear Dr. Ditmars' uncomfortable leggings. We also wore long pants tucked into the leggings, and sun helmets.

The general was one of the finest wing shots I ever encountered; he spotted me thirty years and still managed to wipe my eye several times an afternoon. Leaving his Purdy in Washington, he had armed himself for Liberia with a Browning automatic—twelve gauge, with a twenty-eight-inch barrel and enough choke to make his long shots seem miraculous. Except when damp shells swelled and jammed the mechanism, his Browning was a devastating weapon. One afternoon we flushed a swarm of slate-blue pigeons out of a mango tree, and they took off in every direction. The general mowed down five pigeons with five shots, and the cheers of our naked retainers pleased him as much as the telegram from Cordell Hull at the end of our official Liberian negotiations. Twenty years later, our beaters are probably telling their grandchildren about the general's magic.

For Liberia I carried an old Winchester Model 97 and although my mastery of a pump isn't anything special, I could get off three shots almost as fast as the general could shoot his automatic; my fourth and fifth shots are usually wasted anyway.

We burned up a lot of ammunition under the drenching Liberian sky and every afternoon we brought back a dozen or more guineas, plus as many pigeons as we had shells to invest in the rice fields. Now and then we jumped a wild peacock—an overrated bird on the table and not much fun as a target. But mostly we devoted ourselves to guineas, which were so plentiful that our depredations seemed to make no appreciable dent in the population of the savannas.

All this was observed with interested satisfaction by our colleagues of the diplomatic crops in Monrovia, who began trying to cadge rides with us out to the grasslands. After one incautious experiment when a chargé d'affaires blew a hole in the bottom of our car within seconds after he had assured us that his shotgun was unloaded, we politely declined. Instead, we invited the diplomats to come to the American Legation for dinner.

It was a gala evening, with our colleagues in cummerbunds and white mess jackets and the kerosene lanterns putting an extra gleam on the brass buttons of the legation houseboys. There was breast of wild guinea for each guest, plus Niersteiner 1922 acquired from the Firestone plantation. The rubber magnates laid down their wine when they rented their million Liberian acres, and then found out that their Ohio personnel preferred bourbon and branch water. General Winship and I bought their cellar with the enthusiasm of Pizarro discovering Peru, and the bachelor German minister, who said he hadn't tasted Rhine wine for five years, lit up like a firefly in the firefly mating season.

We had martinis to start with, but the Monrovia ice had to be used the same day as your latest booster shot for typhoid, so I mixed the cocktails in the morning. I put the cocktail shaker, minus ice, in the hiccoughing legation refrigerator, which burned kerosene to produce its chilblains, forgetting that an undiluted martini will melt the gold inlays right out of a deacon. When our guinea hens appeared and were distributed to each diplomat, and the houseboys stood back with their buttons and eyeballs reflecting the lamplight, the ranking guest rose unsteadily and made an unmemorable speech, except that at the end he marshaled his eloquence and stared glassily at his plate, heaped high with the product of our prowess.

"Wild guinea," he announced. "You chop'm fine, mister." Which was to say—Good Hunting!

Doña Mercedes
and the Wild Geese of Patagonia

WHEN THE Nazi pocket battleship *Graf Spee* tangled
with a British squadron off the coast of Uruguay in 1939
and two days later committed inglorious suicide outside
the Montevideo breakwater, the repercussions were pro-
longed and various. For one, German stock sagged throughout the hemisphere. For another, the American government,

sensitive about the Panama Canal, urgently bethought itself about our alternate route through the Strait of Magellan,
which we would have to use if someone dropped a brick in
Culebra Cut or blew up the locks at Miraflores; that the
Graf Spee had been prowling about the Patagonian neigh-
borhood gave added weight to American apprehensions.
For a third, the American government decided to reopen
its consulate at Punta Arenas, on the north shore of Magellan Strait—a windy inhospitable location. And lastly, as a
remote result of these developments, I myself had the
privilege of knowing Doña Mercedes, arbiter of Patagonia.

The United States once before maintained a consular out-
post at Punta Arenas, but in 1915, after the Panama Canal
was opened, a frugal State Department closed the office
and released the wind-blown consul to other latitudes. In
1940, not long after the *Graf Spee* tore herself to pieces in
the River Plate, the State Department selected a recent
Annapolis graduate, commissioned him as vice consul, and
said to take himself to the tip of the continent. He was instructed to rent an office overlooking the roadstead and
report what he could see there, with special reference to
passing ships, their nationalities, and the cargoes they carried. As an afterthought they mentioned Doña Mercedes.

The vice consul duly sailed for Valparaiso. The American
Embassy in Chile was instructed to forward him to his
Patagonian destination, ambition and code books intact, and
to report from time to time to the State Department on his
welfare and progress.

Serving as first secretary of our embassy in Santiago at
the time, I was unaware that this skein of events was likewise drawing me toward the Strait of Magellan. I greeted the
new vice consul in my embassy office overlooking the Plaza
de la Moneda, and I felt paternal. For Patagonia I recommended heavy underwear and diligent performance. I took
the vice consul to dinner at the Club de la Union and sent

him on his way by a Chilean freighter. In due course maritime statistics began arriving from Punta Arenas; these I transmitted to Washington, without comment, for the edification of the Office of Naval Intelligence. Presently there was a letter reporting that between Valpo and Magallanes his freighter had run aground, but that after two days he was on his way again; the vice consul asked that so much of this episode as was consistent with security be relayed by the embassy to a young lady of his Annapolis acquaintance, along with word of his safe arrival in Patagonia. A subsequent letter requested a supply of shotgun shells, twelve-gauge, with heavy loads, number two shot. "The wild goose shooting," he wrote, "is wonderful." We acknowledged his correspondence. These were the kinds of communications that were likely to emanate from a vice consul in possession of his official faculties and not unduly concerned about where the pavement ended.

My ambassador departed on summer vacation, leaving me in charge of United States interests in Chile. In the northern hemisphere, it was the winter of 1941. Hitler was carrying the torch of coexistence with Soviet Russia while Ribbentrop and Molotov argued about stripping the corpse of Poland. Pearl Harbor was still ten months before us. Our consul in Valdivia, a durable citizen who woke himself up every morning with Tabasco sauce, reported that in the heart of the German immigrant district around Osorno everything was quiet; the Chilean hyphenates there, like the German-Americans in Wisconsin, were loyal to the land of their New World adoption.

In Santiago, at the Club de la Union where the young *guasos* of local society had tall drinks at the long bar each evening, the talk was largely of nitrate and copper, booming because of American wartime purchases; of the señoritas at the new Hotel Carrera and of their less inaccessible sisters in the Parque de Santa Lucia; and of the midsummer golf tournament at Los Leones. There was a joke at the expense of the German ambassador, who had unexpectedly encountered his British colleague in the boys' room, but in the main that summer the war blazing over Europe was far away from Chile. This also was the general tenor of my reports to the State Department.

Washington, in contrast, having fixed a suddenly-become-vigilant eye on the Strait of Magellan as the route through which the Atlantic Fleet might one day have to deploy in haste, was eager for all kinds of information. Long cables began to reach the American Embassy in Santiago, to be relayed to Punta Arenas. Urgently they asked about the effect of Nazi submarine sinkings on the stockpile of frozen mutton in the Patagonian *frigorificos*. What of the *estancieros* who came to South America from the Falkland Islands at the turn of the century; could these expatriate Scots be depended upon in the event the Buenos Aires politicians went pro-Nazi? How rose and fell the tides in the Beagle Channel? What of the Chilean-Argentine Rodriguez family, who reportedly owned half of Patagonia and most of Tierra del Fuego? In any case, please send a report about Doña Mercedes.

Reading these peremptory messages, and also wondering about Doña Mercedes, I gathered that all sorts of erudite studies were in progress in Washington, with annexes labeled Tab A and Tab B, all the way down the alphabet. Admirals were establishing deadlines for captains and lieutenant commanders. Wave on Wave supplied stenographic assistance beside the Potomac. But in Punta Arenas on the Strait of Magellan, with the wind roaring up from Cape Horn and his tin stove emitting doleful crepitations and his girl on the Patuxent suspected of dating an ensign, the State Department had only one lonely vice consul, decoding cables by kerosene lantern.

Observing these developments, I was on the point of

telegraphing Washington that much of the desired information could be found in the official Chilean Yearbook, copy on file in Room 315 of the State Department, when the embassy received a cable from the Secretary of State, addressed to the ambassador. This message spoke briskly of the requirement for "full, up-to-date, and authoritative information about all matters affecting the areas bordering the Strait of Magellan," and it directed, in a tone small Washington bureaucrats enjoy using toward their far-flung brethren, that the ambassador designate a responsible officer to proceed from Santiago to Punta Arenas where he would (a) inspect the new American Consulate with particular reference to the political and economic reporting of the vice consul, and (b) see to it that there was prompt compliance with telegraphic requests for information about Patagonia, already transmitted.

It was a crisp directive, and, although I entertained sound doubts whether it had ever been nearer to Cordell Hull than his Division of Latin American Affairs, there the message was, over the signature of the Secretary of State, and not lightly to be disregarded. I took pains not to disregard it. Within the hour, All America Cables had my coded reply, which stated that with the ambassador returning to Santiago next week, the first secretary was departing immediately for Punta Arenas. My reply had a fine ring of efficient public servant leaping eagerly aboard his bicycle, outstripping the message to Garcia. Privately, I was curious about Doña Mercedes. Likewise I remembered the vice consul's interest in shotgun shells and wild-goose shooting. My Model 12 with a thirty-inch barrel was overdue for a workout. I cabled the vice consul saying I was coming.

My young friends at the Club de la Union were pessimistic. Magallanes in midwinter, they declared, is no place to visit. In midsummer February perhaps, when there is a short *temporada* during which instead of freezing to death you only half freeze to death. On the Punta Arenas golf course, if you drive a ball against the wind it goes scarcely ten meters, but when you drive with the wind you have to chase the ball halfway across Argentina. In May, they reminded me, it is practically midwinter; that time of year no sensible *chileno* goes south of Santiago, not even for skiing. As for wild geese, they said, the *estancieros* regard them as vermin.

I set sail two days later on the *Aviles* of the *Cia Chilena Interoceanica de Vapores,* Puerto Montt for Buenos Aires via the Strait of Magellan, a scheduled run down the inside passage of six days to Punta Arenas. And it was on the *Aviles* that I encountered Doña Mercedes.

Meeting Doña Mercedes followed an unfruitful conversation with the Chilean captain who told me as we headed into the Golfo de Ancud that with the señora aboard the voyage might last four or five days longer. When I asked who the señora was and what she had to do with it, he told me that her husband, Don José, now in the Argentine on business, was the owner of the Chilean Interoceanic Steamship Company, specifically the *Aviles,* which he had the honor of commanding. I was annoyed at the delay, for my cabin on the *Aviles* was not to be mistaken for accommodations reserved in advance on the *Queen Mary,* besides which I had consular and goose-hunting business in Punta Arenas. I said so. "We anchor," reiterated the Captain, "at nightfall. Each night before dark, the *Aviles* anchors." And as the winter twilight thickened, the skipper made for a forested shore off the island of Chiloé, and down came the anchor.

After dinner I again waylaid the captain. "What's the matter?" I asked. "Is the señora timid?" His reply was illuminating. "Señor," he confided unhappily, "Doña Mercedes is afraid of nothing, least of all of the water. She swims like a penguin. But she mistrusts nocturnal navigation. Unfortunately she was aboard when the *Aviles* struck an uncharted rock, five months ago, in Desperation Channel. An American consul was also a passenger. There was fog—and you could not see your thumb before your finger. As a result, Doña Mercedes lacks confidence in nocturnal navigation. So we anchor."

So that was the answer. With the Señora aboard we navigated only in daylight, and each night we sought the lee shore, snug as a loon on Moosehead Lake in November. There are worse penalties, for the inside passage has the most improbable scenery south of the fjords of Norway. Meanwhile, after dark, the skipper moodily drank pisco sours, alone in his cabin.

When she failed to appear on deck, I sent my card to Doña Mercedes. She invited me the next evening to the small drawing room outside her cabin. I was prepared for a dragoness, but met a microscopic Diana.

"You are irritated," she told me, "but I find your irritation supportable." She had a crown of white hair and her dark eyes were enormous. "Sailing at night through these narrow channels is dangerous, as I told your vice consul. The tired *Aviles*," she told me severely, "is fifty years old, and the hull is of iron. Ask the captain. With a steel hull, if you strike one of these rocks the water is so cold that the passengers wearing life preservers are the unlucky ones—they endure five minutes longer. But with a fine iron hull when you strike a rock you go *crunch—no hay problema*. You sit there and wait until one of our tugboats from Aysen or Puerto Natales pulls you back into the channel. But it is not wise to stretch the luck of even the *Aviles* too far. Ask the captain."

I sipped my sherry and remarked that I was visiting the American vice consul. Doña Mercedes approved; in fact she spoke well of him and of his conduct when they had sat on the tooth of a ledge, waiting for the tugboat from Aysen, on Doña Mercedes' previous voyage. "A good boy," she said, "if lacking in experience as an official. He even asked me, Doña Mercedes, to spend that time in a lifeboat." She asked if the vice consul was married, and I recalled the message forwarded to the lady beside the Patuxent. No, I said, I thought the vice consul was single.

"Too bad," said Doña Mercedes. "That American girl lacks spirit or she would have accompanied him to Punta Arenas."

This I found a refreshing point of view after the tepid attitude in the Club de la Union. I said as much, but added that nevertheless the young women of Maryland stood high in American estimation. Doña Mercedes sniffed. She tapped a tiny slipper on the floor of her *sala.* "You have curiosity," she said, "about our backward Patagonian civilization?"

I confessed that the region interested me, and I mentioned the emigration to Patagonia from the Falkland Islands.

"I suppose," said Doña Mercedes, "it is because of the war you wish information. I too believe that the war will soon afflict the United States, and that Chile will not escape it. Patagonia already suffers because ships no longer come for our mutton. About the people from the Falkland Islands . . ." The señora said they were the best sheep farmers in the world—tough as the oak trees twisted by the wind above her family cemetery in Punta Arenas. "Also," she remarked, "they drink a great deal of whisky." She said her husband, Don José, confirmed it; these Scots brought whisky with them in barrels from the Falkland Islands—which she called Las Islas Malvinas—half a century ago, when she was a schoolgirl in Punta Arenas. She regarded me alertly over the rim of her sherry glass. "One of them wanted to marry me. Papa sent me instead to the Convent of the Sacred Heart in Buenos Aires."

Doña Mercedes spoke of her girlhood beside the Strait of Magellan. The unfenced pampas was empty then, with the grass pressed flat by the steady cold wind from the South Pacific. She made you feel it. One summer, she said, her mother built a lattice of wood, six meters high, and planted sweet peas and summer vegetables, shielded from the wind. But the fence blew down, and Papa was furious. "He had something there in a box under glass—mint, you call it—which the people from the Islas Malvinas use to flavor their mutton." She said the Scotchmen laughed, but that Papa was very angry. "But do not believe," she said decisively, "that today their children are not loyal chilenos." Her small voice rang, and there was conviction in it.

Thus the *Aviles* moved slowly south, and each night we anchored in the lee of an island. The small voice of Doña Mercedes tinkled like a silver bell, gay, wise, and unpredictable. I asked her about the shooting. That was to say, the *cazeria*—the hunting. At first Doña Mercedes was puzzled. I explained that this was a North American heresy; I didn't mean sea lions, or guanacos, or Alcalufes, or ostriches; I said I was interested in wing shooting. Wild geese, I said; I had heard there were many.

Doña Mercedes regarded me with dark bright eyes, crinkled with amusement. "Señor," she said, "in Patagonia we are sheep farmers. Three wild geese eat as much grass as one sheep, in addition to spoiling our pampas. Wild geese are without utility among us. If you wish to shoot geese, you are a public benefactor and your only preoccupation will be the ammunition. Let me know upon which of my *estancias* you wish to conduct the extermination."

The next afternoon we reached Punta Arenas. The long line of the Andes, marching south for three thousand miles, was at last waist-deep in the antarctic smother. Bitter scud blew over the open roadstead from behind Tierra del Fuego. The roofs of Punta Arenas were corrugated iron, tight at the eaves, and a three-story building was a Patagonian skyscraper. Fortified by farewell pisco sours, poured by the Chilean skipper who looked forward to navigating twenty-four hours a day north from the Strait of Magellan to

Buenos Aires, I came ashore by launch, in the wake of Doña
Mercedes. The waves froze on the gunwales.

Looking enthusiastic and young, the vice consul presented me to Chilean officials. The mayor, a nephew of
Doña Mercedes, said in Oxford English that if the captain
of the *Aviles* hadn't forgotten to put aboard his consignment of Booth's gin at Valparaiso, he looked forward to
pouring me an early martini. I said I looked forward to
sharing one with him. The intendente said I was a long way
from Santiago; I gathered he was a fugitive from the Club
de la Union and wished he were back there. The commanding general, in a long gray coat with gold at the shoulders,
said he hoped my trip had been comfortable, and he added
that the American vice consul was a stout man on horseback—beyond which, between Arica and Cape Horn, there
is no more friendly recommendation from a citizen of Chile.

In an animated group on the pier, Doña Mercedes was receiving assembled relatives, who were calling loudly upon
favorite saints to witness her safe arrival. The *Aviles* skipper
would not have enjoyed it. We paid our respects and Doña
Mercedes poked me with a mink-mittened hand. *"Señor
Diplomatico,"* she said, "I wish you good hunting." And she
cocked a bright, friendly eye at my bachelor vice consul.

Ashore in Punta Arenas, with the windows of the consulate
rattling, it took me all of one hour to establish that the
American representative farthest south was competently
supporting the interests of the United States in uttermost
Chile. The vice consul's fee stamps were in order; his safe
contained his consular seal, together with his code books and
other official oddments as prescribed by the regulations; his
classified correspondence was accounted for; and, notwithstanding Washington carping, his reports seemed to be
current, even including data on the rise and fall of the tides
in the Beagle Channel. His office was tidy and on the sill
next a window was a pair of Navy binoculars trained on

the harbor where the *Aviles,* with a wisp of smoke shredding from her stack, looked small and deserted. On a packing box beside the vice consul's bed was an alarm clock and the picture of a girl—a girl with the quirk of a smile and questioning eyebrows. Clearly this was the lady of his Patuxent correspondence.

I said my official piece and the vice consul seemed pleased. It took an additional ten minutes to ascertain that the next ship from Punta Arenas for Valparaiso left sixteen days later. Between now and then, I said, I'd examine his reports in detail, as well as give him some pointers on keeping the Washington civil servants soothed in the future. As before with the vice consul, I felt paternal. And then I turned my attention to hunting. With the British Consulate down the street, equally supplied with binoculars capable of surveillance over the harbor, I said there was no reason why the American vice consul should not make a deal with his British colleague, and then accompany me to one of Doña Mercedes' *estancias.*

"Five months," I said, "is long enough to spend in one place, even if it's Punta Arenas. While I'm here we'll do a piece on the wool clip. In Washington they haven't thought of that yet, and a voluntary report will impress the home-office statisticians. You need a vacation."

I expected enthusiastic assent but to my astonishment the vice consul withheld his endorsement. More surprising, he looked far from happy. "Sir," he said, "I'm sorry I can't go with you." He turned pink to the ears and looked younger than ever. "I mean," he said, "I have a previous engagement."

After fifteen hundred miles in ten days, dangling each night from the *Aviles'* anchor, I was in no mood for official malingering about unofficial business. Before I left Santiago I had telegraphed news of my impending arrival—and also of projected hunting. I revised my estimate of the vice consul. For once, I thought, Doña Mercedes might be mistaken. A promising young man, but evidently going to seed on this, his first assignment. A disappointing development.

"What do you mean?" I demanded. "That you can't take a week's leave to go shooting? You've earned it. Do you think I came all the way to Patagonia just to watch you brush your teeth and balance your fee stamps?"

The vice consul shook his head. He looked very unhappy. During an embarrassing silence I mentally transferred him to Valdivia and planned to send the Tabasco-sauce consul from there to Punta Arenas. Anyone who took red peppers before breakfast should do well in Patagonia.

"You see, sir," said the vice consul suddenly, "it's this way. I mean that it isn't that I don't like to go hunting. This is the best place in the world for wild geese. I'd like to go with you. It's only . . . You see, sir, it's my girl, sir. My girl reached Buenos Aires last week. She's due in Punta Arenas on one of Doña Mercedes' ships next Sunday. We expect to be married. . . ." He was looking at the picture on the packing case beside his alarm clock.

I congratulated the vice consul. I told him sincerely that I was delighted. I added that wedlock was admirable. When I was married, I said, I was myself a vice consul. It isn't where you are, I remarked; it's where you are going. I returned my estimate of the vice consul to its original location, and the eyebrows of the photograph on the packing case seemed to approve my decision.

Presently the vice consul accompanied me to the Hotel Cosmos, where he left me. My luggage was intact, including my long-barreled shotgun and the ammunition to shoot geese with. The Hotel Cosmos advertises itself as *El Hotel mas al Sur del Mundo,* with a luggage label featuring an emperor penguin admiring an orange antarctic sunset. Juan Toth, the proprietor, secured the blinds, with the air of a man who doesn't expect to undo them before springtime in

October. A hot bath was called for, and likewise a whisky and soda. I had them and felt my spirits rising. There was a telephone in the room and I decided I needed to talk to Doña Mercedes.

At her house several people intervened, but presently there was her small remembered voice, this time with laughter in it.

"*Hola, amigo,*" said Doña Mercedes. "I thought you'd be calling. When I reached home there was a cable from Don José, in Buenos Aires, and he says things about your vice consul's *novia* which if he were not sixty-nine years old and my husband, I might find offensive. I said your vice consul is a good boy, and that his American señorita should be a young lady of spirit. She will be very welcome in Punta Arenas."

There was a pause, while Doña Mercedes considered. "Sunday," she said. "They do not have to anchor at night between the River Plate and Punta Arenas. The ship should be here on time. But there will be legal formalities. I shall speak to the mayor, my nephew. I think the wedding can be Tuesday. For three days, *Señor Diplomatico,* you can chase your wild geese. You will not be needed. And also, if you are not frozen, you can chase wild geese after the wedding. I shall respond for the arrangements. There will be a reception. . . .

"You see," she continued, "we esteem your vice consul. And furthermore," Doña Mercedes told me warmly, "there is war coming. It will be a bad war and I do not like it. Here we may not be attacked but there will be many difficulties and privations. It will be good for the people in Punta Arenas to see that Chile and *Norte-America* are friends and allies, from the very beginning. I shall be responsible," she declared, "for all the arrangements."

I told her, rather feebly, that all this was altogether too spontaneous and generous. I said that as the representative of the American Embassy in Chile I also ought to be up and doing.

"Pouf," interrupted Doña Mercedes. "Next Tuesday you can give the bride away. If I know the young man, he will think that sufficient. But wait, you are right. There is one thing more. Young people are hungry. Even when they are in love they are hungry. You can help with the wedding breakfast. Roast goose will be a formidable contribution. Roast wild goose. Get on with your shooting. . . ."

Against my further observations, Doña Mercedes had an abrupt patriotic answer. "If your wild goose is as tough as I think it will be, the bride and groom can always eat our good Patagonian mutton, *Señor Diplomatico.* Good night— and good hunting!"

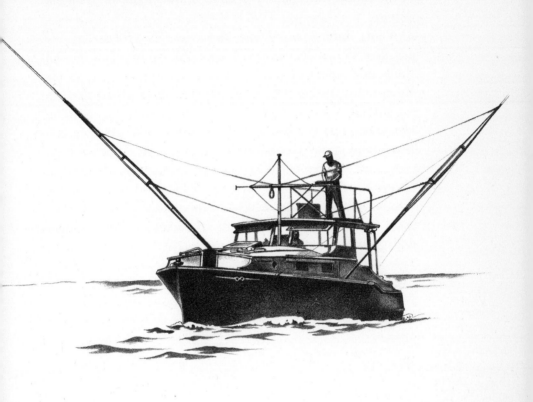

No Hasta el Postre—Meaning You Can't Throw Rolls until Dessert

THIS IS a story of how Ernest hunted for Nazi submarines off the coast of Cuba in the dark days of World War II, and of how he grew his impressive suit of whiskers, first a manly brown but now gone whitely patriarchal. But especially this records how we lured Ernest back from unrewarded vigil beside the Old Bahama Channel to attend his own birthday party in Havana: a stirring festival featuring an obstacle shoot with shotguns, and a mixed bag of targets and contestants. We ate roast pig thereafter, and the dessert was a long time in coming.

Pearl Harbor found us unprepared in more areas than the Pacific. In Cuba we had a four-million-ton sugar crop coming up, an island dependent on ocean transportation, and few defenses. Soon we had merchant seamen straggling into Havana daily, red-eyed survivors of torpedoed ships, plastered with fuel oil and molasses. At the Hotel Ambos Mundos they were sorted out by the naval attaché and flown to Miami.

The Cuban people were all for the war, but they wanted to be convinced we were fighting it. The prime minister of Cuba declared that if we didn't get an airplane over Morro Castle—just to show the flag and let the *cubanos* know we still remembered the *Maine*—he couldn't vouch for the temper of his fellow citizens. Our government finally sent a flotilla of fishing boats from the Florida keys, owners and crafts hastily commissioned in the Coast Guard Reserve, with depth charges like fifty-gallon gasoline drums lashed to the stern. Although they didn't destroy any Nazi submarines, the flotilla made a comforting display at anchor in Havana Harbor. The prime minister of Cuba perked up when they got there.

It wasn't until seven months after Pearl Harbor that the United States Navy got its first Nazi submarine in the Caribbean, but by that time U-boats were lurking in half the inlets along Cuba's sixteen-hundred-mile coastline.

A new American ambassador came to Havana. He was as competent as he was large and indestructible—characteristics which commended him to Ernest, who had been doing volunteer work for us on land while he cursed the submarines and our inability to cope with them at sea.

Ernest's project started with a discussion of how Count
Luckner of the Imperial German Navy foxed the Allies in
World War I by disguising a sailing ship as a Norwegian
fishing boat. We spoke also of the British Q-boats that
looked like tramp freighters until the false bulwarks fell
away and the guns started firing.

"There's my fishing boat, the *Pilar*," said Ernest. "Around
Havana everybody knows the *Pilar*. Why can't we convert
the *Pilar*, and make like a Q-boat? When a submarine comes
up and signals us alongside, we'll throw hand grenades into
the conning tower."

We elaborated the scheme one night in the embassy, and
Maria, the ambassador's wife, appeared now and then to
remark that the clock was pushing tomorrow. "What we
need," went on Ernest, unheeding, "are hand grenades.
Could you help us there, Mr. Ambassador?"

Ambassador Spruille Braden thought maybe he could.
He'd talk to the naval attaché about it. He did so, and cables
were dispatched to Washington. A week later Colonel John
Thomason of the United States Marines visited Havana. He
twirled his eyeglasses on a black silk ribbon, and the decora-
tions he wore were not the kind you get for flying across
a war theater between one staff job and another. He and
Ernest were friends of long standing.

"I don't say it's impossible," said the colonel. "Only crazy.
That conk of yours on the noggin, Ernest, must have addled
your porridge."

"That," pointed out Ernest, "is probably what King Priam
said to Ulysses when Ulysses dreamed up his Trojan horse.
Say on, my Colonel."

"How big a crew can you put on the *Pilar*?" asked the
colonel. "And where do you expect to cruise? Even accept-
ing your premise that no Nazi skipper is going to waste a
torpedo on anything so small as the *Pilar*—suppose your

submarine surfaces and then instead of ordering you alongside so you can throw beanbags down his hatch—suppose
he stands off and blows you and the *Pilar* out of the water.
What then, Papa?"

"If he does that," replied Ernest, "then we've had it. But
there's a good chance he won't shoot. Why should a submarine risk attracting attention when the skipper can send
sailors aboard and scuttle us by opening the seacocks? He'll
be curious about fishermen in wartime. He'll want to know
what kind of profiteers are trying to tag a marlin in the Gulf
Stream with a war on. If he recognizes the *Pilar*—so much
the better. Carry enemy sportsmen back to Berlin to write
dirty limericks about the Führer. Feather in bonnet for der
Kapitan. Fame and promotion for the crew. Why not? Those
boys are suckers for publicity."

"But even if you get ordered alongside," argued the colonel, "your Nazi skipper isn't going to pipe you aboard to
have a glass of schnapps with him. He'll have men on deck,
and they won't be holding slingshots."

"That's right," admitted Ernest. "Along with the grenades,
we need a machine gun. I shoot a machine gun good, John.
Practiced on my grandmother. Standard equipment for a
Cuban revolution. Nazi sailors won't know what hit them.
Now how big is the conning tower and how wide is the
hatch? But what I really want to know is, how much damage
would grenades do inside a submarine?"

"Plenty damage," conceded the colonel. "Submarine full
of sensitive gadgets. Wouldn't care for it myself. Might even
put a U-boat out of commission." John Thomason upended
his tumbler and Ambassador Braden refilled it. "Way we're
losing ships in the Caribbean, sure would give us a lift if
you pulled it off, Ernest." But the colonel shook his head.
"Your scheme is too simple, Ernest. I'm telling you, as a professional sailor. If you find a submarine, chances are you'll

crawl out the small end of the cornucopia. U-boat surfaces—
Pilar goes pouf!—exit Papa."

"Fine," said Ernest cheerfully. "That's what I wanted to
know. Only drawback is, I'll miss the winter bird shooting.
Now about a crew. I've got Wolfie . . ." and he named the
name of a nine-goal polo player who had drifted into Havana. "And I've got two Cuban sailors."

"Cubans?"

"Sure, Cubans. *Good* cubanos. It's their war too. I'll respond for the Cubans."

So that was how Operation Friendless—named for one of
Ernest's black cats at Finca Vigía—got started. Alterations on
the *Pilar* were undertaken at Cojimar, over the ridge from
Havana. Thence rum runners sailed during the prohibition
twenties. People don't talk at Cojimar, and from there to Key
West is ninety miles across open water. There were other
arrangements, sponsored by the embassy. Grenades arrived.
A radio was installed and also a collapsible rubber boat,
bright orange, with aluminum oars. Machine guns were
forthcoming, and the naval attaché was busy commuting
between the embassy and Ernest's headquarters at Finca
Vigía. Documents were presented to Ambassador Braden,
for not even in wartime do the assets of Uncle Sam change
hands without the signing of papers.

And with the weapons and equipment, Colonel Thomason,
as a parting contribution, sent Ernest a professional volunteer
—a master sergeant of Marines with sixteen years of enlisted
service behind him, and a bottomless thirst for *definitivos*
ahead of him. In the dark the sergeant could take a machine
gun apart in a matter of seconds, and put it together again
while you reached for a cigarette lighter. By hand, he could
traject a grenade in a calculated parabola and drop it into a
barrel four times out of seven. He was a lovely uninhibited
character, and he brought us a farewell note from his colonel,

who was clearing his Washington desk and heading for the Pacific.

"Good hunting, Papa," wrote John. "Give my love to Admiral Doenitz."

Under the sergeant's coaching, Ernest's crew became dead shots with hand grenades. Whenever other chores besetting the counselor of a busy wartime embassy permitted I used to drop around, and sometimes I made the mistake of sampling Ernest's evening *definitivo*, a homicidal brew in a tall smoking glass, the exact ingredients of which were as closely guarded at Finca Vigía as the Bacardi rum formula in the family vault of Pepin Bosch at Santiago de Cuba.

Wolfie complained of throwing his shoulder out the first day, and never getting it back again. He wanted to know why Mongo and Mario, Ernest's two Havana *jai alai* confederates, couldn't come around and teach the crew to throw grenades out of a *cesta*. The sergeant took aboard a bushel of comic books while Ernest shipped the raw materials for *definitivos* and some yellow pads on which he wrote an eloquent introduction to *Men at War*. "Only thing I regret," said Ernest at a farewell briefing, "is that Operation Friendless washes out my winter bird shooting."

They got away from Cojimar one cloudy night in February 1943, in high spirits.

The *Pilar* cruised from Bahia Honda clear to the Old Bahama Channel. There was nothing amateur about Operation Friendless, and never have five men—alternately broiled by the tropic sun and drenched by the Cuban offshore dew—worked with more dedicated purpose. Trouble was—no submarine. Ships were torpedoed, almost within sight of them, but the U-boats didn't wait on the *Pilar's* coming. The *Pilar* caught marlin, and that was as the disguise demanded, and it rescued American seamen. But the *Pilar* was hailed by no surfacing enemy submarine.

The crew came ashore from time to time, down the island. Ernest reported to Havana by telephone—deliberately obscure messages that spoke of a murderous sunburn and referred to logistic problems. "The cat needs hair tonic" was, after some cogitation, interpreted to mean that Operation Friendless was low on *definitivos,* whereat an ensign from the naval attaché's office was dispatched to Nipe Bay with what we guessed might be the principal raw materials.

We were wrong about the ingredients, but we had as a dividend the reappearance of the *Pilar* off Cojimar, an interlude that got Wolfie back to Sans Souci where the rumba orchestra makes a man forget that the oncoming dawn will stab shards of broken mirror into his eyeballs. It got the sergeant to Dos Hermanos Bar on the Havana waterfront, where he met three bulldozer operators from Brooklyn; they were carving out a Cuban airstrip at five hundred dollars apiece a month, and they proclaimed the rigors of their war effort. The sergeant, wearing a *guayabera* shirt and discontented over the absence of submarine targets, came into action with a bottle of Arechebala in one hand and a bar stool in the other. Principe Prison housed him overnight, and the local *beneficencia* did about the disabled bulldozer operators.

Ernest spent his leave with his two youngest boys and had a report of hunting on the south coast—moonlight hunting for the long-shanked fulvous tree duck the Cubans call *yaguasa:* you shoot against the moon at a whisper of wings and you chase the cripples by flashlight while mosquitoes lift you straight out of the warm mud by the ears. Hunting *yaguasas,* it pays to have DDT and atabrine handy.

At the embassy, Ambassador Braden went over the *Pilar*'s log with the naval attaché, and we took stock of the submarine situation. The Caribbean score was still a grim reckoning, but clearly the odds were changing. We had escort ships now, with radar, instead of lonely freighters heading

for destruction. Blimps floated over the convoys. Bombers were replacing the single-engine jobs at San Julián, guarding the Yucatán Channel.

Ernest, rubbing cheeks burned raw by the wind, admitted that Operation Friendless was becoming obsolete. He'd give it one more whirl and then sign up as a war correspondent in Europe. Try growing a beard this time to protect his face from sunburn—maybe whiskers were lucky. "My crew is OK," he reported. "I've got Wolfie reading Renan; he's doing all right except he keeps looking in the back of the book to find out what happened. The sergeant has graduated from comics to *Time* and *Newsweek;* he's developing politically. The fishing has been good. My Cuban *viejo* really talks to the marlin. Absolutely! When Friendless folds, I'll do something about him. And anyway, it's too late in the season for any more bird shooting."

Of all the sacrifices to Operation Friendless, Ernest missed most his bird shooting: the explosive rise of quail, with the covey streaking away toward the nearest cane field; the quick evening flight of slate-blue torcaza pigeons coming to roost at the edge of impenetrable *manigua;* the fragrant dawns when, scalding coffee and scrambled eggs under your belt, you took the Carretera Central to the east of Havana, night merging imperceptibly into day, palm fronds dripping diamonds in the first sunlight, and soft blue hills between you and Mantanzas.

Thus the Cuban spring and early summer. The American ambassador in Havana concluded that Operation Friendless, still without issue, could go into mothballs—the rear admiral in Miami regretfully concurring. Since Friendless was a classified project, official recognition was limited at the time to a warmly appreciative letter from Ambassador Braden. This was supplemented after the war by the public thanks of the United States Navy.

Even though the *Pilar* took no Nazi scalps for the trophy room at Finca Vigía, we of the skullduggery department— rear-echelon manipulators and correspondingly reckless— were reluctant to see the *Pilar* beached without further demonstration. Ernest's impending birthday provided the peg on which we hung our ministrations. In his honor we invented a havoc that was known before the event as Operation Friendless' Brother. This debacle was named for another of Ernest's Finca Vigía cats—an animal that stayed up a ceiba tree for three days after the termination of the celebration.

Several of us belonged to a shooting club in the vicinity of Ernest's house. It was called Club Cazadores del Cerro— Hilltop Hunters Club—and whether Ernest bought his finca because it was near the club, or whether the club was organized because it was near Finca Vigía, was never established. Club Cazadores was a Cuban institution with a single criterion for membership: devotion to shooting, with shotguns. Every Sunday during closed season on quail and ducks and pigeon and wild guineas, that is to say from April to September, members converged on Club Cazadores, some of them still in evening clothes from the Casino Nacional, with lipstick on their righthand lapels, but all of them bearing shotguns.

At Club Cazadores you shoot clay pigeons of a morning—trap or skeet as the impulse assails you—and you shoot *tira pichón*—live pigeons—in the hot Cuban afternoon.

Tira pichón is a noble sport even though in the United States it exists in clandestine insecurity, along with rooster fighting and the conversion of good American corn into bad American moonshine. The S.P.C.A. turns a bloodshot eye upon it. In *tira pichón* you mark out a three-quarter circle, with a fence two and a half feet high around it. A grandstand with a roof of *yagua*—the thick upper fronds of the royal palm—protects the spectators from the summer sun, and the kibitzers are articulate and critical.

In the center of the open space enclosed by the fence, which is over fifty yards across, are five launching machines, sunk in the ground and arranged in an arc. Each sunken trap consists of an arm on a spring, with a container the size of a fifty-perfecto cigar box at the end of the arm. In each container is a live pigeon. It is the same principle that gets a *jai alai* ball out of the *cesta;* the same principle that throws an apple off a hardwood stick, with the speed multiplied in proportion to the length of the arm.

The hunter stands behind the arc of traps, facing forward, and as he moves up to the firing position he spins a roulette which drops a ball into one of five slots, controlling the launching mechanism. When the hunter shouts "Pull," a live pigeon is thrown from one of the five traps, so separated in their arc as to provide a margin of uncertainty—as with a bird flushed in a field. In *tira pichón* you have two shots, and to score the pigeon must be downed within the circle of the fence. If you knock down the pigeon with the first shot,

the second shell can be used to make sure your bird doesn't revive and fly away from the small boy who acts as retriever.

This shooting is more difficult than it sounds, partly because of the capriciousness of the wind, but mostly because pigeons are stupid and hence unpredictable. As a naturalist has observed, pigeons are the most sordid vertebrates unplucked; to use them as shotgun targets is to treat them better than, left to themselves, pigeons treat each other. However, this is no moral treatise and it is submitted merely that shooting pigeons out of a trap ranks with putting worms on a fishhook—the S.P.C.A. kindly take notice.

Thrown in the air, a good pigeon will make off at top speed. Although it isn't the world's most difficult target, a pigeon is capable of carrying number six shot beyond the limit of the encircling fence, and a bird falling outside is counted as a miss. *Er-rr-rado!* A missed pigeon is so unintelligent that it often circles back, perching in one of the mango trees on either side of the grandstand, like as not starting to coo and make love to another survivor thirty seconds later.

The machine tosses a pigeon fifteen feet in the air, and one in four will immediately drop back to the ground, not bothering to open its wings. This is a trick shot because the hunter is tensed for a rising bird and if the pigeon touches the ground before the shot is fired, that counts as a miss. *Er-rr-rado!* Many arguments take place at Club Cazadores over these dropping birds, and the possibility that instead of flying the pigeon will take a perpendicular fall contributes to hasty shooting and many misses.

The members of Club Cazadores pack the premises every Sunday afternoon. Ten birds per contestant make a match, the hunters withdrawing after the second miss because otherwise with twenty-five guns the performance would run into the sudden darkness of the tropics. The National Championship is held in August, with relatives and *queridas* on hand and extra bartenders, and that shoot lasts all day— twenty birds to a man, only those killing twenty pigeons in succession being eligible for the elimination shoot-off.

Ernest's youngest boy, Gigi, was runner-up at the age of eleven, last *Campeonato Nacional* before Pearl Harbor. He stood in the sun all day, barefoot, shooting a twenty, against the best shots in Cuba, shooting twelve-gauge pumps and automatics. His twenty-eighth pigeon, cleanly killed but far out, hit the fence and bounced over. *Er-rr-rado!*

World War II, by making it difficult to obtain ammunition, put a crimp in Club Cazadores. Julito, a trustworthy scoundrel who manned the traps and loaded the live pigeons into the cigar-box containers and who lovingly oiled our shotguns while he swindled us on *globos,* became morose and dispirited. A pigeon turned imbecile is a *globo.* Instead of starting for the nearest horizon or dropping back to earth, it hovers over the trap, resentful at being awakened. Generally speaking, *globos* don't prosper, but I have seen a crack shot miss one, both barrels, and retire to the accompaniment of Cuban bronx cheers, which are loud and uncaressing.

Before hostilities in the Caribbean began, Ernest and his assimilated companions used to take over Club Cazadores on weekdays for practice sessions and secret experiments with *definitivos*. The war and Operation Friendless deprived Julito of both revenue and hangovers, so that when we approached him with a proposition for a birthday shoot in honor of the Principal Patron of the Institution, he lit up with the enthusiasm of a broker, expecting a visit from the district attorney, who is invited instead to float a public utility issue. In short, Operation Friendless' Brother engaged his immediate attention. Julito offered to contribute six pigeons, guaranteed not to be *globos,* from his private collection, and in exchange for a small additional consideration he agreed to tamper with the roulette mechanism of the traps to the end that not even Peps Merito, Marquez de Valparaiso and champion of *tira pichón* at Monte Carlo, could knock down a fluttering *globo*.

Ernest's sons offered valuable suggestions. Why not have an obstacle shoot, with targets other than pigeons? They knew a man in Batabanó who had a covey of quail in captivity. Score five if you kill your pigeon, deduct five for a miss. Double the points for quail. And at Finca Vigía the boys also had half a dozen untamed *yaguasas*. We decided theirs was a fine idea, and we elaborated upon it.

Meanwhile Ernest steered the *Pilar* back to Cojimar, where he combed out his glistening whiskers. He still had no Nazi submarine, but it had been a dedicated effort. He paid off the Cuban boy and he discharged his Cuban *viejo*. The Marine sergeant, awaiting assignment to the First Marine Division which was about to invest Saipan and Tarawa, fell into further adventures that attracted the unfavorable attention of the authorities. We bailed out the sergeant with monotonous regularity and the naval attaché decided the sergeant was developing too fast, politically.

We assembled, at length, the most unorthodox collection of targets ever set before shotguns. In addition to the pigeons, the birthday offerings included the covey of quail and the six tree ducks from Ernest's sons, along with a half bushel of Cuban oysters with mangrove streamers on each shell, a dead guinea pig, seven clawless lobsters, and four small tuna. Constantino, the bartender at the Floridita, contributed an immense *cangrejo moro*—a moro crab—with protuberant eyes and an uncompromising expression. And Mongo and Mario, Ernest's two *jai alai* players, brought us a basket of pelotas—the balls that thud each night off the walls of the *frontón*—their most treasured possessions. Mongo and Mario were forthwith added to the guest list, over the sergeant's objection.

We got ourselves to Club Cazadores soon after the *Pilar* was decommissioned on Ernest's forty-fourth birthday. Our guest list was complicated. Ernest's friends if laid end to end—after sampling *definitivos* for example—would have reached all the way from Cabo San Antonio to Guantánamo. His local admirers included maraca players, sugar-mill owners, taxicab drivers, priests, deep-sea fishermen and small fry from the American Embassy. Screening the list of guests eventually reduced itself to a must-know basis, with Ambassador Braden commanding me to express his regrets: he had an important engagement, he declared, two weeks from Tuesday.

The *blanco gordo*—that is, the main target—we agreed would be the immense moro crab contributed by the Floridita Bar, and that would be fair enough considering the hours the guest of honor and his companions had spent there. With extra tension on the spring of the trap we estimated the crab would fly fifty feet in the air and make a surprising target, especially since Ernest would be expecting a pigeon. The crab would be saved for Ernest's last shot, and it would count twenty-five points if he chipped the stone-hard carapace. If he hacked off a claw or disintegrated the crab with his load of birdshot, his score would be doubled.

The sergeant was appointed referee of the shooting. With a rifle he could hit a dime at one hundred yards, and he could nick it more often than not with a forty-five-calibre pistol, but he didn't know one end of a shotgun from the other. We figured this made him an expert at our special brand of *tira pichón.* If not, we said, the pellets would rattle off his own shirt front. This was a good idea. But as a secondary responsibility we put the sergeant in charge of the *definitivos.* That was a bad idea, for the sergeant took an immediate dislike to the *jai alai* players, Mongo and Mario. He muttered throughout the afternoon of cooling them, a phrase from the *Pilar* expedition which Ernest invented to describe what happens to a gaffed marlin when the club hits it behind the bill, and the eyes as big as dinner plates go suddenly cross-eyed. As the *tira pichón* contest wore on, the sergeant was restrained with mounting difficulty from tangling with Mongo and Mario.

Word of the shoot got around, as such things do in a country where no revolution can succeed until all the principal protagonists have whispered so loudly of their designs that most of them have been jailed before R (for Revolution) day approaches, and we had the inevitable gate-crashing problem. The owner of a sugar mill, who cheated with slot machines, was thrown out, along with two members of the Havana Yacht Club, who vowed the Pearl of the Antilles would ring with the infamy of our conduct. On the other hand we let in a fraudulent Polish count, recently acquitted of murdering his father-in-law in Jamaica, Ernest insisting that if you had been placed in peril of your neck by the British Raj, and then turned loose after defense testimony so damaging that no amount of imagination could be equally incriminating, there was no use trying to make an alligator-skin bedroom slipper out of a count's ear. This was a metaphor so engaging that we pressed a double *definitivo* on the discredited laird of Crackow and hailed him to the firing line with shouts of "Tira, mata suegro" (Your turn, assassin of father-in-law), and he shot better than most of the invited contestants.

Ernest's whiskers elicited comment. It was variously asserted that he resembled Ivan the Terrible, Amy Lowell, Santa Claus, and the south end of something going in the opposite direction. Only Wolfie was philosophical about Ernest's whiskers. "Papa knows best," he declared simply.

The archives of Club Cazadores yield no statistics of that birthday tournament, which Ernest won by acclamation after Julito substituted for the giant moro crab a five hundred-watt electric light bulb. Ernest popped it, fifty feet in the air, and instead of the ears and tail of the bull we voted him a Daisy air rifle, payable out of the treasury of the Havana Yacht Club. Wolfie, who shoots better than all except two per cent of the amateur hunters the world over, was disqualified for clipping a *globo* missed in two easy shots by the Marquez del Merito. Wolfie said it was an accident—he was reaching for a *definitivo* and just happened to pick up a shotgun.

Nobody shot a quail; the entire covey was probably back, pecking at cracked corn in Batabanó thirty miles away, by sunset. But when Julito threw out a handful of oysters, with the mangrove bark trailing after, the sergeant took two quick shots at them with his pistol. In the ensuing scuffle he lost the pad and pencil with which he was supposed to be scoring.

The survivors, as the velvet Cuban sunset stained the horizon, made a pattern of footsteps toward Finca Vigía, where Ernest's cook was trying to keep Friendless and Friendless' Brother out of the birthday cake while he put the finishing flames against the *lechón asado*—a roast pig contributed by the fishermen of Cojimar.

At Finca Vigía the sergeant brewed up a fresh batch of *definitivos*. Wolfie tasted one and recoiled, stricken. That gentle giant wiped his eyes and observed to Father Andres that someone must have put razor blades in it. Ernest was incensed. "Don't put in razor blades," he admonished. "You'll weaken the *definitivo*."

The table was set beneath a great ceiba tree that must have been there when Christopher Columbus was still His Most Christian Majesty's Admiral of the Indies. There was difficulty with Mongo and Mario, whom the sergeant with an eye to protocol seated at opposite ends of the table, thirty feet from each other. Deprived of their *cestas,* they hadn't hit anything all afternoon with shotguns; they were looking for trouble. "I'd like," said the sergeant to Ernest, "to cool those pingpong-playing fairies." He looked around for a likely implement.

"Basques," said Ernest severely, "are noble people. No Basque can do wrong at Fica Vigía."

"Sez you," muttered the sergeant.

Father Andres was asked to say grace. A peasant priest from Andalusia, he rose with a dignity that matched the purple Cuban night and the stars shining through it. A silence came upon Ernest's birthday gathering, and in that silence you could hear the grease sizzling under the roast pig and the hungry mewing of Friendless and Friendless' Brother. Father Andres told of what makes a man a man, and he said you don't always measure achievement by what happens in headlines—the heartline is often a better measure of victory. I don't think he knew of the cruise of the *Pilar* but what he said made us glad to have had some small part in it. We remembered John Thomason, for word had come that he wouldn't be returning from the Pacific. We thought of all the empty hours the crew of the *Pilar* had spent on the

Gulf Stream, tensed for a moment that did not come—a moment of high endeavor.

What time our padre was speaking, the unrepentant Mongo was tucking away another *definitivo*. His gesture lingered over the table, and his hand—the sinewy hand of a professional *jai alai* player—closed over one of the hard-baked rolls that the neighboring village of San Francisco de Paula makes daily for Havana consumption. They are as solid as duckpins and about the size of a baseball. Mongo picked up one of those rolls. With one hand he automatically acknowledged the padre's benediction while his other hand, biblically dissociated from spiritual proceedings, drew back from the table.

As Father Andres sat down, Mongo's roll shot out with the flat trajectory of a recoilless rocket. It went through the lower third of Ernest's whiskers like a humming bird through a thistle and it traveled the length of the table with enough more than the speed of light to set up a new theory of relativity. The sound of that roll taking Mario on the top of his still-bowed pate was the plunk of a baseball bat connecting with a watermelon.

Mario roared like a sea lion deprived of a five-pound bonito. Lurching, he climbed to his feet almost as quickly as the sergeant. The sounds of hissing grease beneath the roast pig and of hungry cats sampling the feast were no longer audible, while far down the horizon the Southern Cross blinked at the doings at Finca Vigía.

"Lemme at those fairies," pleaded the sergeant. "One-two, and I'll cool them for you." The sergeant breathed through his nose; here was something the Marine Corps knew about. Something more profitable to a sergeant than casually encountered bulldozer operators. "I'll cool them for you, Papa," he repeated.

Ernest came slowly to his feet. He dominated the sergeant and he dominated the table. Toward Mongo, who had thrown the roll, he extended an arm like a tree trunk, an arm furred to the wrist, with a hand the size of a ham at the end of it. He opened his hand and shook his finger, first at the sergeant and then at the two *jai alai* players.

It was a menacing gesture. Guests who were still taking cognizance of things gathered themselves before the storm. A hurricane was obviously brewing. What was left of Ernest's whiskers bristled. Lightning appeared to dance about the head and shoulders of Moses.

Then Ernest remembered that he had just declared that no Basque could sin at Finca Vigía.

"That was wrong," declared Ernest mildly. He picked up another of the rolls from a pile in the center of the table, the mate to the roll Mongo had thrown at Mario. He balanced it in his hand, like a baseball. "That was wrong," Ernest repeated. "On my birthday you can't throw rolls until dessert. *No hast'el postre!*"

Pokey and the Chungking Flying Bat Sweepstake

IN CHUNGKING, in 1945, we were all very busy winning the war—or so we thought at the time—and Chungking was a dismal place. Straddling a red sandstone ridge at the junction of the Chialing and Yangtze Rivers, over one thousand miles from the sea, Chungking became the wartime capital of China precisely because of its inaccessibility. Pat Hurley was American ambassador when I arrived in China but he was off on a special mission to Moscow, where Stalin described the Chinese Communists as "agrarian reformers." Molotov went "Da, da!" meaning Uncle Joe is always right.

At the end of the number two priority that stretched from the Potomac across North Africa to India and Burma, the Air Transport Command set me down at Chiulungpo, the muddy airfield of the Nine Dragons of Chungking, in March of 1945. My host conducted me through alleys redolent of things casually buried in the time of frost, now answering to Szechwan spring. At dinner that night he served me bitter salted peanuts and martinis made out of Chialing gin, which he said was distinguishable from Chialing vodka because the gin had less sediment in it. This was the first accurate information I received about China.

In the months to follow Chungking was to produce indelible impressions. It is no part of my chronicle to speculate on how we lost China. Ours were more immediate preoccupations: Ambassador Hurley's Cadillac for example—Pat's pride and joy in diplomatic achievement—and a great tribulation to the rest of us. Another was a dinner party four Chinese generals gave in my honor; the generals introduced me to a potable horror called *baigar*. And a third was a shooting tournament that took place on the veranda of an Air Force general's house in Chungking, a project known as the Flying Bat Sweepstake.

In these and other activities I was sustained by a large American Marine whose name was Pokey. Henry Clay Polk —hence Pokey. A hunting friend of other days, Pokey had recently been commissioned a first lieutenant and forwarded by the Marines to China. He arrived, with credentials, a few days after I did. Unlike most of us in Chungking, Pokey flourished.

Chungking living was full of harassments. What wasn't reduced to rubble by Japanese bombing was constantly catching fire as the survivors huddled around their cooking pots in the ruins. We dwelt in a house that was trying to slide into the Chialing River, with an assist from each succeeding rainstorm. The electric current gave only a flickering yellow light and after dark it was hard to read chancery documents. Pokey discovered that if you screwed a one-hundred-ten-volt bulb into a Chungking-current socket, the filament took on new life; it glowed bravely for three or four hours before burning out, and that was as long as Chialing gin (or vodka) permitted you to stay awake anyway.

Up and down the hill from us lived senior American Army officers, each of their houses with an electric generator of its own. So when anyone in the embassy needed a shave, Pokey used to tap a general's line. This led to many popped fuses and scorched generals, to the detriment of military-diplomatic relations.

When asked how he came by the one-hundred-ten-volt bulbs and the tapping equipment, Pokey said Naval Stores, out on the edge of town, just happened to have those things handy.

Ambassador Hurley's Cadillac was a more complicated problem. When Pat reached China, the embassy rolling stock consisted of a 1938 Mercury sedan driven into China over the Burma road after seeing hard service with General Stilwell, and a vintage Chevrolet flown over the Hump and crash-landed on arrival. The Chevrolet had a list to starboard and the doors on that side couldn't be opened. There were also three rickshas, all with bent axles.

Hurley examined these relics without enthusiasm. He said that if you could straighten out the bent axles in China, that would be more good than the Lend Lease Program. Pat then declared, vehemently, that if he had his way Lend Lease would be suspended long enough for him to buy back with the proceeds enough new Buicks supplied to cabinet members and diplomatic representatives of our Allies to furnish the American Embassy in Chungking with adequate transportation. Lacking State Department support for this worthy project, Pat commandeered from the Army a covey of jeeps for the chancery, and for himself a Cadillac limousine originally destined for Lord Louis Mountbatten's headquarters in Ceylon.

That Cadillac was an elegant chariot but, like many other things brought to the wartime capital of China, it languished when it got there. The car had an automatic drive that demanded operation at upwards of thirty miles an hour, whereas through the quacking Chinese crowds filling Chungking streets, five miles per hour was extravagant progress. The innards of the Cadillac were forever burning out, frequently in the wake of General Wedemeyer's three-star jeep, to the elation of the military and the indignation of the American ambassador.

Hurley left orders, when he flew to Washington several weeks before my arrival in China, that on his return to Chungking he damn well expected to find his Cadillac in perfect condition. There the matter stood when I got there. There it rested until Pokey took over. Pokey volunteered to tow the Cadillac behind a weapons carrier, four hundred miles south to the motor pool in Kunming, where a light tank could be cannibalized to make a new stomach for it. That miracle performed, Pokey himself piloted the Cadillac back to Chungking in state, taking salutes on the way from officers up to and including full colonels. And on the return trip Pokey loaded the Cadillac with household supplies worth almost their weight in gold in our isolated city. Pokey also provided transportation for several personable young women who worked for Bill Donovan's organization.

Asked how come he found the weapons carrier to tow the

Cadillac to Kunming with, Pokey replied that he just happened to have a weapons carrier handy. The OSS girls, he added, just happened to be in Kunming in need of transportation.

Pokey solved the problem of Chungking living by assigning himself to an assistant naval attaché of the embassy, who was our chancery doctor. Pokey's official business had to do with the rescue of American airmen downed on the Asian mainland, inside the Japanese lines. That was a project not at the time susceptible of public discussion, so it was given out that Pokey was on a medical mission.

Our Naval commander was a man of nocturnal habits. His activities involved us in protracted litigation with the Military Police, who were trying to enforce the curfew. It went against the grain of the MPs that the embassy staff, enjoying diplomatic immunity, couldn't be arrested. The MPs took resentful notes which were forwarded to the embassy by the provost marshall's office, through channels. Pokey's name was regularly included because our commander, who treated embassy personnel by day, frequently treated Chinese patients at night—Pokey going along as observer and companion.

Sample MP report: "At 0315 [three-fifteen a.m. as civilians write it] Amembassy jeep 14 stopped by Cpl Witherspoon. Jeep occupants two naval personnel [here names and serial numbers of the commander and Pokey] and two female civilians, indigenous. Officers showed diplomatic accreditation and jeep allowed to proceed. . . ." I used to pacify the provost marshall by telephone and tear up the summonses.

Thus Pokey enlarged his horizons, and prospered. He called our excellent medical commander The Quack. In addition to driving the doctor's jeep, Pokey learned to sterilize instruments and on occasion to calculate blood pressure and take temperatures. Between them, Pokey and The Quack made more good will in Chungking than a dozen official pronouncements from Washington. Likewise Pokey proved impervious to fatigue and exposure, so when presently I needed a secret weapon to employ on four Chinese generals, our Marine lieutenant was again elected.

The Chinese generals belonged to the era immediately following my arrival in China. In my honor they gave a dinner which proved something of a disaster because neither my predecessor, who took off for the United States as soon as I was installed, nor the Old China Hands who remained to advise me, bothered to explain the custom of *gambeying*—much less how to guard against it.

At a Chinese dinner the hosts and guests embark upon a protracted exchange of toasts. Drinking only rice wine, served in little cups, *gambeying* is an innocuous custom, especially if the boys' room isn't too far from the table. A *gambey* calls for draining the cup, that is to say, bottoms up—after which the cup is held out, upside down, to prove you haven't cheated. Later in the evening the cup is held over the head of the drinker, for the same purpose. For Chinese, who can tidy up by passing a damp cloth over their shaven heads, a round of *gambeys* is no problem, but for foreigners with their hair still intact, *gambeying* calls for a shampoo before bedtime.

The correct defense against *gambey* is not to reply *gambey* in return, but to say *swaybien*, which relieves the answerer of having to go bottoms up. *Swaybien* allows him to sip his cup honorably instead of draining it.

None of this was explained to me in advance, nor was anything said about two further gimmicks. My Chinese generals did not serve rice wine. They served *baigar*, a lethal distillate. *Baigar* compared to Chialing gin (or vodka) is like a charge of gunpowder beside an eyedropper of conjunctivitis medicine. Secondly, the generals didn't drink *baigar*—at least not after the first few courses; they drank cold tea out of a separate but identical container. But they filled my cup, again and again, with the genuine throat-searing article. After several hospitable hours of this, I was escorted home making noises like a red squirrel, the generals acquiring much face and the dinner party counting as a fine success—for the generals.

With a head like a hollow tree buzzing with hornets, I summoned my colleagues the next day for a conference on strategy. They recommended that, after a suitable pause, the generals be invited to a return engagement. At the second dinner there should be an equal or preferably an even greater number of dishes. If the generals were *gambeyed* under the table by the end of that meal, face would be restored and the honor of the embassy vindicated.

That was where Pokey came in. The generals were duly invited. No cold-tea subterfuge was employed at our dinner. We drank our *gambeys* even. Our number one houseboy did us proudly with supplies Pokey brought back from Kunming in the Cadillac. The generals were durable and their chopstick technique was on a high professional level, but the generals had never lived in Kentucky.

After the fifth course I replied *swaybien* to my guests' *gambeys*, and I sipped my cup instead of upending it. But all the generals got out of Pokey was *gambey*, and again *gambey*, and more refills. By the ninth course several generals were surreptitiously helping themselves from Pokey's supply, hoping it was tea, and then blinking like freshly landed Yangtze carp when they realized it wasn't. By the fourteenth round, the survivors were gasping. By the eighteenth, Pokey and I were alone at the table.

Word got around Chungking that honors were even. Sino-American relations were correspondingly fortified. Asked how we did it, Pokey modestly pointed to the commander's medical cupboard. As a dividend from the Kunming Cadillac expedition, Pokey explained that The Quack just happened to have a case of 100-proof bourbon handy.

Following that triumph Pokey organized the Pink Elephant Society, but the MPs remained unsympathetic, and members had difficulty getting home. Pokey was called away from Chungking for several weeks on business and the town was a smaller place without him. Thus the Szechwan spring wore on, while victory came to the Allies in Europe and the perimeter surrounding the Japanese islands shrank under the pounding of our Navy and Air Force.

In honor of V-E Day the Russian Embassy in Chungking, uncooperative in other particulars, staged a mastodon reception, with caviar flown all the way from Astrakhan in a Lend Lease C-47. That was the first time I heard the American ambassador give his Oklahoma Indian yell; the sound so shattered Pat's Soviet colleague that he almost took off from Chungking for Siberia without looking over his shoulder.

But on the whole Chungking did not improve on further acquaintance. We sweated and choked, while prickly heat frayed our tempers. We set ourselves and we took it. Meanwhile Pat continued to negotiate with Uncle Joe's "agrarian reformers," his Washington instructions pointedly demanding that Embassy Chungking promote the unification of China. For several days we had Communist leader Mao Tse-tung from Yenan, below the bend in the Yellow River, on a visit to Chungking under safe conduct. Mao wore a natty Sun Yat-sen jacket and 1920 model golf knickers but his notion of Chinese unification—reiterated the following year to General Marshall—was that if the American government would bank the game, Mao would oblige by furnishing loaded dice and calling the turns. Neither Chiang Kai-shek nor Ambassador Hurley was buying any.

General Wedemeyer's army was training Chinese divisions. The Air Force in our sector maintained the over-the-Hump supply route and protected Chungking against diminishing Japanese air raids. Hiroshima was only two months away, but none of us sweltering in Chungking was party to that grim foreknowledge. We recognized, however, that the center of the war had moved to the western Pacific.

To our fliers I turned in hopes of arranging a few days of leave, with bird shooting up the Yangtze River where we heard of curlew and snipe in the meadows on the edge of Tibet. Bustards were mentioned, and pheasants. Nothing came of that either, except that I fell in with some equally frustrated hunters with whom as a substitute for Tibet we proceeded to organize—while the Potsdam Conference occupied the attention of statesmen in Europe—the Chungking Flying Bat Sweepstake.

The Flying Bat Sweepstake contributed little toward winning the war, but with Pokey's assistance it almost rendered me solvent. The house of an Air Force general commanded a view up and down the Chialing River, there nearly a mile wide, swirling with viscous brown eddies. The sandstone cliff dropped off sheer below the house, one hundred feet to a mud shelf occupied by the owners of sampans. The general's third floor veranda, running the length of the house on the river side, enjoyed a late-afternoon breeze. It was a civilized spot in wartime China and thither I often repaired at the end of the day to exchange tall tales of hunting in happier latitudes.

The notion of shooting bats was the inevitable result of the ingredients thus assembled. In the half-hour before twilight there emerged from the caves and crannies of the sandstone cliff below the general's house hundreds of small flying creatures, taking their one-a-day meal from the insects that rose off the scalding margin of the Chialing River below us. Noiseless except for the whisper of naked wings, they swooped and swirled around the veranda, six feet from the railing one second and a hundred feet over the river two seconds later. If we neglected to spray DDT around, the bats ventured almost into our ashtrays. And as night thickened and the red went out of the western hills toward Chengto, the bats were gone as suddenly as they made their appearance—back to their caves, where they hung upside down, waiting for tomorrow's flying and eating.

The Air Force, it developed, had access to shotguns. Early in the war the idea took root in the Pentagon that shooting a shotgun makes a man more accurate with a weapon mounted in the tail of an airplane. The Air Force decided it approved of shotguns. As a result, fliers received a generous ration of training items labeled "expendable." Their pumpguns weren't Purdys, and the stocks were too short, but they discharged their skeet loads and for a man brought up on quail in the South or woodcock in New England, an evening bat on the wing, with the light fast fading, was no amateur's target. In short, the pumpguns sufficed, and the shells were all on the taxpayers, kindness of General Chennault and the over-the-Hump airlift.

After several evenings of desultory bat shooting, we decided to organize the contestants. Since the things you could spend money on in Chungking were limited to bingo sponsored by chaplains and to such extracurricular activities as escaped the vigilance of the Military Police, the Flying Bat Sweepstake underwent a rapid expansion of scope and horizon. The idea, that is to say, caught on. From a group of half a dozen enthusiasts diluting their Chialing gin (or vodka) with powdered lemon juice and lukewarm water, the enterprise generated several score clients, all clamoring to get in on the act and willing to put dollars on the line for the privilege of doing so.

The coolies living below the cliff, along the margin of the Chialing River, were no less enthusiastic. A boiled bat, the coolies reasoned, is a tasty dish; so why not encourage the Mad Strangers in the useful pursuit of free victuals? Nothing, literally nothing, is without utility or value in China.

If left to themselves the bats rarely ventured out of their

caves before sunset, thus affording us a scant half hour of shooting before darkness descended. But we found that if we offered a small reward to the coolies, they would organize teams of youngsters, letting them down the face of the cliff in baskets. By exploring the caves and poking into the sandstone crannies with sticks, the boys induced the bats to fly out an hour earlier. This arrangement allowed us to enroll additional contestants. It simultaneously swelled the day's bag of bats, which is what our coolie friends believed we were there for.

Bats are extremely erratic in flight, and one of the problems was to devise a system whereby a consensus was obtained that a given shot was "dead" or "miss." None of the bats was ever retrieved—the coolies saw to that—so there was no sure way of satisfying the optimistic gunner who declared, heatedly, that *his* bat had crumpled in midair and fallen as dead as yesterday's mackerel. We solved this by enrolling a special corps of spotters, keen-eyed and (we hoped) incorruptible. Inasmuch as the words "dead" or "miss" contain no Ls or Rs, we taught the spotters to shout those monosyllables in a sufficiently intelligible chorus to be understood by the colonel-of-the-day, who with bookkeeping apparatus manned a second-floor window, just under the veranda. The word of the spotters as interpreted by the scorekeeper was ruled to be final.

With the cooperation of an Air Force brigadier general who knew about horseracing, we devised a parimutuel system and the Air Force machine shop at Paychee constructed a tabulator and an elegant scoreboard, with spaces for names of contestants—win, place, and show—and the odds dependent on the amount of the betting. That scoreboard was an elaborate contraption, mounted on two telephone poles sunk in cement in the garden. I have often wondered how the Communists, capturing Chungking three

years later, interpreted this capitalist relic. If they understood horseracing they were probably puzzled, for a two-
acre plot of broken ground at the top of a cliff lacks the
attributes of a jockey club or a racetrack. I hope some
Marxist archeologist spent a lot of time trying to figure out
what the scoreboard was there for. He can relax if he reads
this story.

We had more sweepstake applicants than we could possibly satisfy. Having participated in the project since its
inception, I was able to veto the idea that rank be an
entrance criterion; my plans included the presence of
Pokey who, as a Marine first lieutenant, would have been
bounced right out of the tournament. Qualifying rounds
were also discarded and it was decided that after a certain
number of Air Force candidates were accepted the remaining places would be rationed among the other armed services,
plus the embassy. That was a benevolent gesture toward
diplomacy which the aviators later regretted, but it enabled
me to get Pokey's name on the list, inconspicuously, near the
bottom of the scoreboard. His inscription was accomplished
during an altercation with our parimutuel expert, who maintained that we ought not to call it a sweepstake unless we
sold numbered tickets. The Air Force engineers retorted that
that would make their homemade tabulator, whereof they
were proud, too complicated. We called it a sweepstake
anyway, and Pokey's name was accepted as an embassy
candidate, without anyone's taking particular notice.

The shoot was scheduled for the first Saturday afternoon
in August. Pokey got back to Chungking two days before
that important Saturday, having covered half of non-occupied China by jeep, sleeping in verminous *hans* and dodging around in the rice paddies when he found himself too
close to Japanese outposts. The Quack prescribed disinfection, followed by malted milk spiked with Chialing gin (or

vodka). Pokey took this advice, in reverse order. He then consumed a steak flown from Australia and a bowl of rice half as large as a bathtub.

And what, Pokey wanted to know, had we been up to, during his absence?

I had borrowed one of the Air Force shotguns. I showed this to Pokey. I described the sweepstake and summarized the regulations. He was instantly delighted. But when he put the gun to his shoulder the stock was so short that Pokey's cheek rested against the barrel, well forward of the breech mechanism. He could shoot the gun one-handed maybe, like a frontier revolver, but if he kept the butt against his shoulder it would clearly not be much more effective than waving a roman candle.

Pokey furrowed his brow and considered the problem. "Know anyone in Chungking," he inquired, "with a man-sized shotgun?"

The Quack and I had thought of that too. We'd canvassed the town and the results were negative.

"How about OSS?" asked Pokey hopefully, naming Bill Donovan's outfit.

"We tried that," I told him. "They've got personnel mines, midget machine guns, and fountain pens that go off in your cornflakes. I asked Quentin Roosevelt. He says—no shotguns."

"A pity," said Pokey. Suddenly his face lighted up and his blue eyes sparkled. "The OSS!" he exclaimed. "Bill Donovan's babes. They can fix it!" Pokey went rummaging in his room and came back with his oversized Mae West over his arm. He started for the door with the life jacket and shotgun.

"Don't tell anyone," I shouted after him, "that you've ever been shooting."

Pokey made no response. Presently the alley rocked to the sound of Pokey's departing jeep. Through the diminishing

commotion came the thin startled cries of our Chinese neighbors seeking refuge up trees and in the shelter of doorways.

Our lieutenant returned several hours later in triumph.
His girl friends of the Kunming Cadillac safari had evidently
stopped whatever they were doing for OSS long enough to
engage in feminine efforts with scissors and needles. The
canvas cover of Pokey's life jacket was a sacrifice to the
Flying Bat Sweepstake, and the kapok stuffing, much com-
pressed, was now the inside of a boot, five inches long,
which made a solid extension for the short stock of his
shotgun. Two inches of additional canvas fitted snugly over
the butt, with eyeholes for a shoelace that, drawn taut,
kept the extension from slipping. It was a professional job
that Abercrombie and Fitch might have envied. The girls
stenciled Pokey's initials in green ink on the outside of
the orange canvas cover. It would doubtless have been
just as easy to have our Swatow carpenter whittle a wooden
piece to splice on the stock, but as The Quack pointed out,
that wouldn't have been as much fun for the girls.

So the Saturday of the sweepstake arrived. It was a gray
stifling day with no breeze to ruffle the parched shrubbery
around the edge of our Air Force general's garden. The
river bank below the cliff was already lined with expectant
Chinese wearing round conical hats and cotton drawers.
Someone had thought to outfit our small boys with blue
nylon shirts and they looked very gay squatting near the
rim of the cliff beside their coiled ropes and their bright
straw baskets. Various other factotums were in white, red, or
yellow, depending on their functions. I suspected more
scissors and thread at work, this time in the dismember-
ment of Air Force parachutes.

It was not in my program to enter the competition. Aviators were out of my class. When calibrated for bat shooting,
the twenty-twenty eyesight that spots you a Zero and then,
as the enemy pops out the other side of a cloud, brings your

guns to bear at several hundred miles per hour, is too large a handicap for a diplomat. I was on the committee charged with looking after foreign guests—fellow diplomats and Chinese officials.

It was my intention, nourished since the sweepstake was initiated, to collect some easy money by betting on Pokey. I looked forward to the proceeds not only to set against losses sustained during earlier shooting with my Air Force colleagues but likewise to acquire a Chinese painting I coveted. My betting scheme was simple. Pokey had been away, and no one in Chungking except me had ever seen Pokey at work with a shotgun. Moreover, it was a general's house and most of the entrants were field grade or higher; colonels and generals don't pay much attention to footloose lieutenants. The size of the entrance fee further discouraged the juniors. The drinks were for cash too, the profits if any to be applied to one of Madame Chiang's charities.

All in all, betting on Pokey looked like an airtight proposition. I had seen him shoot partridge and *tortolas* in Chile, and I'd hunted wild guineas and ducks with him in Cuba. A skill like Pokey's lasts as long as the hunter. I planned to wait until shortly before the gong and then place my bet with The Quack's dispensary orderly, one of several enlisted men serving the ticket windows. Even if my bet reduced the odds on my candidate, Pokey should still be a profitable long shot. His skill ought to pay fifteen or twenty times my investment.

It was a sound plan. I had a place on the wall already picked out for my Chinese painting. I hoped Pokey hadn't told anyone what he could do with a shotgun.

The Flying Bat Sweepstake was well attended. The diplomatic corps turned out, along with Chinese officials. Pat Hurley, immaculate in a blue sharkskin suit and his elegant white mustache, was conspicuous among the bush jackets and shorts of the service contingent. The ambassador declined a reserved seat and went off to have beer with the newspaper correspondents. The boys started needling him about the "agrarian reformers" and when I heard the AP correspondent ask, "But Mr. Ambassador, aren't you making a molehill out of a Mao Tse-tung?" I shuddered. Pat was quick on puns, and the ambassadorial boiling point was low. His Indian yell, intended to put the Associated Press in its corner, instead flushed a premature cloud of bats from the side of the cliff. They circled around us for several minutes, adding to the general air of sweepstake expectancy, and then the bats decided it was too early for events and flew back to their upside-down nap before sunset. Lieutenant General Sir Adrian Carton de Wiart, V.C., came with a British contingent. He was Winston Churchill's personal representative in China. His red-and-gold cap sat jauntily over his black eye patch and his single hand held a swagger stick. "This," said Sir Adrian, "is what I came out to China to witness."

My four Chinese generals arrived, full of geniality. I led them to the bar while they proclaimed, "Hao! Ding hao!" meaning they were pleased to be present. When I offered them drinks they said, "What—no baigal? No boulbon?"— meaning, What, no baigar or bourbon? and they patted their stomachs. We settled for iced tea laced with Chialing gin (or vodka) and I propelled them in the direction of the ticket windows. All Chinese, I reflected, are inveterate gamblers.

I placed my own bet shortly before the deadline. My one hundred dollars brought down the odds on Pokey to twenty-three to one, and as a craven afterthought I put an additional twenty-five dollars on Place and Show. Then the gong sounded. The small boys in blue nylon shirts jumped into their baskets on the edge of the cliff, shouting and shaking their rattles. The baskets were lowered down the sandstone escarpment, and the Chungking Flying Bat Sweepstake was on.

There were thousands upon thousands of bats, and whenever they became discouraged the boys were lowered another ten feet in their baskets to the next cave, where they flushed a new crop of targets. Down on the river bank, under the cliff, there were some of the most spirited fights among coolies since Genghis Khan disbanded his army. Sampans crowded inshore and the naval engagement was equally spectacular.

Since the contestants were shooting identical shotguns, each man was issued five shells at a time. He could load them in his pumpgun singly, with a pause after each shot to listen for the tally, or he could fire at will, as fast he could, like a hunter behind a rising covey. The only stipulation was that no contestant could shoot at bats close in; any falling bat that failed to clear the edge of the cliff was automatically counted a miss.

My Place and Show bets, as I look back upon them, were disloyal. Henry Clay Polk won that tournament with less effort than it takes to put it to paper. There were two doubtful moments when he missed his third and fifth shots, but he polished off the next five for an eight out of ten on the first round, which was ample to stay in the running. After that, Pokey borrowed a duck-billed cap to keep the lowering sun out of his eyes, and he wasn't even headed. He had a perfect score on the next two strings of ten each, and he finished with twenty-eight out of thirty. Pokey emptied his gun almost as fast as he could work the forearm. Twice he had three bats in sight at once, all falling. The runner-up, a B-29 pilot with a star over his wings and four rows of ribbons, shot twenty-four out of thirty. The Quack later remarked that it was like stealing Easter bunnies out of an orphan asylum.

As I elbowed my way toward the ticket window I decided

for the first time that summer that Chungking had its own compensations. At twenty-three to one, my one-hundred-dollar investment would net me two thousand three hundred dollars. My Chinese painting was as good as on the wall. There would be enough left over for some jade I'd been offered. Even the Place and Show tickets would add to the kitty. I passed Ambassador Hurley, tearing up a bundle of tickets. "I was robbed," he remarked with his fine Irish grin. "In future, I'll stick to fishing."

At the window I put down my tickets. The sergeant was affable. In exchange for my one hundred dollars to win, he pushed across the counter three one-hundred-dollar bills —total three hundred dollars. I waited, and, when nothing further happened, I mentioned that he still owed me two thousand dollars. "I'll take them in hundreds too," I said. "More convenient."

A chill came between us. The sergeant gave me the hard look of a professional soldier. "Two thousand bucks!" he exclaimed. "What's eatin' you, Mister? You had one hundred dollars on Lieutenant Polk. At three to one, that makes three hundred dollars, and I paid you. Look at the tally."

I looked at the tally, that fine mechanical scoreboard put together in the Paychee machine shop by the Air Force electricians. Pokey's name was there for Chungking to see and admire. Pokey, the winner. But where I had read "23 to 1" after I had placed my bets and gone back to sorting out arriving officials, the tabulator now showed the winning odds not as "23 to 1" but as "3 to 1."

I saw something else as I turned back to the sergeant and his neat piles of money. At the next window were several of Pokey's OSS girls. And just beyond them were my four Chinese generals. They were all engaged in exchanging tickets for money, and the generals were obviously on the receiving end of a substantial transaction. As I limply picked up small change for Place and Show to add to my three hundred dollars, the happy generals came over, waving packets of American currency.

"Pokey shoot velly fine," they declared, beaming upon me. "Pokey velly fine shot. We go now, dlink baigal."

The Chinese generals had cagily waited until the ultimate moment before the gong. Then they bet five hundred dollars apiece on Pokey to win. The odds on Pokey dropped from twenty-three to one, to three to one, and each of the generals thriftily tripled his money.

The generals towed me back to the bar where I numbly accepted a half-tumbler of "baigal." "Gambey," said the generals. I was still dazed by the evaporation of my profits. "Gambey," I echoed mechanically. Then, as I choked and turned purple, the four Chinese generals beat me companionably on the back, full of friendship and high good humor. "Pokey shoot velly fine," they repeated.

That evening I accused Pokey of perfidious conduct, and of treachery unbecoming the dignity of the United States Marine Corps. "I told you not to tell anyone you could shoot," I delared angrily. "By not keeping your trap shut, you ruined my racket. You cost me two thousand dollars."

A bewildered Pokey denied it. "I didn't say anything to the OSS girls," he said. "When I left the house to get the gun fixed, you yelled at me, 'Don't tell anyone you can shoot,' so I didn't. All I told the OSS girls was that I wanted my Mae West cut up to make a boot for the stock, so the gun would fit me. That's all I told them. And anyway," said Pokey defensively, "the girls only bet ten dollars apiece. They said I'd saved them that much by bringing them from Kunming in the ambassador's Cadillac."

"I'm not talking about your OSS girls," I retorted, more irritated than ever. "They're wonderful girls. If they knit you a muffler, I hope you choke in it. What I'm talking about is your telling those four Chinese generals. How else could they have found out you can shoot? Each general bet five hundred dollars. Their bets made the odds drop to three to one. Instead of a long shot, you started the sweepstake the favorite. You and those four Chinese generals cost me two thousand dollars."

"Is that so?" said Pokey sympathetically. He stared at the ceiling. Arithmetic was hard for him. "But those bets were the generals' own idea," he said slowly. "They must have been. I don't even know the generals' names. I haven't seen them since the night we *gambeyed* them under the table with The Quack's case of I. W. Harper."

Suddenly Pokey smiled an infectious grin. It was the grin of a man at peace with his conscience; the warm grin of Henry Clay Polk who made more friends for us in China than a dozen Washington pronouncements; the grin of Pokey, who found a pearl in the oyster of Chungking living.

"I guess maybe the four Chinese generals just happened to think betting on me might turn out to be a good investment," said Pokey. "I guess maybe it was just Chinese intuition."

The Chungking Flying Bat Sweepstake was the only tournament we held in China. Bruised but plotting a comeback, the Air Force scheduled a handicap meet for the middle of August. The bats—and the coolies—were as eager as ever, and with the rating the aviators proposed for Pokey he would have had to shoot more bats than the number of shotgun shells they were going to give him.

But at that point the Japanese, to paraphrase Pokey, just happened to surrender. In Chungking, World War II was over.

How to Shoot Non=Communist Pheasants in Czechoslovakia

SHOOTING PHEASANTS in Communist Czechoslovakia is strictly for the Kremlin pot, but the commissars, with an irony possibly unconscious, maintain the old Hapsburg protocol that used to go with the imperial shooting. The Communists now invite diplomats to kill their pheasants because they regard shooting them as harvesting a valuable crop— pheasants, not diplomats—and because while over the years the comrades have developed some skill with machete, meat ax and machine gun, the intricacies of wing shooting, which most Communists consider a decadent capitalist sport anyway, are generally beyond them.

Thus the foreign diplomats stationed in Prague receive each autumn a formal invitation for *MM. les Ambassadeurs* to proceed to the old Hapsburg hunting lodge at Zidlochovice, bringing two twelve-gauge shotguns per diplomat, plus eight hundred rounds of number six ammunition. Shortly after arriving in Prague as American ambassador, I received such an invitation.

The village of Zidlochovice lies in the Moravian plain, about one hundred fifty miles east of Prague and sixty miles north of Vienna. The battle of Austerlitz was fought just beyond the Zidlochovice oak forests, and Napoleon probably had roast pheasant and Danube grape jelly on the morning after his victory. Archduke Rudolph established the present estate which, after his death in the arms of Marie Vetsera, passed two generations ago to his imperial brothers. King Alfonso shot there often, and the high score for pheasants killed on a single day by a single hunter was made by the late King Carol of Rumania. All the Hapsburgs took their indoor and outdoor sports with serious purpose.

The main hunting lodge at Zidlochovice is built on a scale approximating a Chicago railroad station, and is almost equally draughty. In the halls there are more mounted stags, wolves, capercaillie, deer, foxes, pheasants, and *javorina* than you are likely to encounter inside the Museum of Natural History, and in the bedrooms there are life-sized paintings of callipygian nudes, in the Rubens (or Hapsburg) tradition. Three hundred and forty pairs of roebuck prongs decorate the dining hall alone, not counting the chandeliers made of interlocking antlers. These treasures were augmented after the Communists seized Czechoslovakia by a plaster bust of Marshal Stalin, just inside the main entrance, flanked on the other side by a stuffed four-hundred-fifty-pound boar. Uncle Joe wears a benevolent expression, but the boar looks as though he had just been elected to the Politburo.

After arriving at Zidlochovice in the late afternoon of a gray November day, I surrendered my matched pair of Cogswell and Harrison shotguns to an ancient forester who must have dated back to the days of Emperor Franz Josef. There were nine of us in the party, all foreign diplomats from Prague, and the tenth man was our Czech Foreign Office host with a permanently preoccupied expression. He was responsible, so it turned out, for Arrangements and Decorum.

We were routed out at six o'clock the following morning by the forester's trumpet, and under his tolerant eye I put on my Austrian hunting suit of gray wool trousers with a green stripe down the side, and matching jacket adorned with deer-horn buttons. This elegant costume was surmounted by a green velour hat with a shaving brush aft. I likewise had a fine olive-green overcoat with loose shoulders and sleeves, bought from the Messrs. Lanz of Salzburg. That coat replaced, with misgivings on my part, the scuffed brown hunting jacket with the capacious game and ammunition pockets purchased years ago from Abercrombie and Fitch and thereafter profitably employed all the way from Cuba and Patagonia to Peru, Liberia, and Czechoslovakia. I decided I looked like a fugitive from a Viennese light opera, and how, I wondered, was I going to lug around two shotguns, to say nothing of nearly one hundred pounds of ammunition?

Our Foreign Office representative had breakfast laid on, and he made a speech in French while the gray daylight of European autumn sifted in among the staghorn chandeliers. He gave us directions for the hunt, and we were told not to shoot hen pheasants except as specifically authorized, and not to spin around in our tracks to take rear shots, no matter what the target or provocation. Breakfast over, we trooped out between the bust of Uncle Joe and his side-kick the snarling stuffed boar, and we embarked in three dilapidated imperial barouches, horse-drawn, apparently last painted during World War I.

The Zidlochovice estate produces forty thousand pheasants a year, and thus far the Communists haven't figured out a way to put stakhanovites to work among the already eagerly mas-culine ringnecks. The estate has both fields and forests. Sugar beets, potatoes, cabbages, corn, and turnips grow on the rich farmland. There are wide stands of golden Czecho-slovak oak, which make the finest wine casks in the world. They likewise provide marvelous pheasant cover.

Half an hour from the hunting lodge we were surrounded by three hundred Moravian farmers armed with sticks—our beaters. Thirty government foresters were in command, but among them I identified a substantial covey of Secret Police in brown belted raincoats, felt hats à la Jimmy Stewart, and city shoes already caked with red Moravian mud. The Secret Police, with nobody to arrest because diplomats have diplomatic immunity and cannot be arrested, seemed frustrated and uneager.

Three personal retainers were assigned to each hunter. The first was my gun bearer, who cradled one of my shot-guns under each arm and declined to surrender either of them. The second lurched heavily under several hundred of my Churchill shotgun shells from London, slung in a leather bag over his shoulder. The third was a boy sprouting his first whiskers, unburdened by anything else except the stub of a pencil and a small white pad with my name on it. His function was to keep score of my hits and misses—a disquieting prospect for any hunter.

The hunters rallied around and the chief forester made a

speech, which our Foreign Office friend translated: the first episode would be a two-mile walk through a stand of oaks, jump shots at flushed birds, cock pheasants only. Hares and rabbits could also be killed, and foxes if we saw any. Roebuck and *hirsch* were forbidden. If we flushed a boar and anyone put a charge of number six shot into it, the government of the Peoples Republic of Czechoslovakia would not be responsible for the outcome; next of kin, nevertheless, would be notified. And now, if *MM. les Ambassadeurs* would please deploy to their stations, the proceedings would commence to be unraveled. One moment please: shotguns only; the Argentine consul general would kindly surrender his revolver.

We dispersed and under guidance from the foresters spread out across a quarter-mile front. Ahead of us stretched ten dark lanes through the forest, one lane to each hunter. The lanes were assigned according to rank—the middle ones for ambassadors, with ministers, attachés, consuls, and secretaries on the outside. The lanes were about ten feet wide and a gunshot apart; in the woods between each lane, and therefore between each hunter, there were thirty beaters pounding the oak trees, shaking down acorns, and making a tremendous clatter. Behind each hunter walked his three retainers—the gun bearer, who also loaded each weapon as fired, the ammunition bearer, and the scorekeeper. Behind the retainers, for my special benefit, walked three members of the Secret Police, their feet making squdgy sounds in the moist oak leaves.

The chief forester lifted his trumpet and blew notes that reverberated bravely across the Moravian plain. My bearer accepted two shells from the keeper of my ammunition. He inserted the shells, snapped shut the breech, handed the gun to me, and the whole line moved slowly forward. It was the first time I had touched my shotgun since reaching Zidlochovice.

Before we had moved ten yards, a cock pheasant exploded under my feet and made off, straight ahead of me.

"Cock, shoot! Quick, shoot! Shoot cock quick!" yelled all three of my retainers. So did the three Secret Policemen.

I raised my gun. With a baseball bat I could have given that pheasant a permanent headache. I fired both barrels. The pheasant, shedding no feathers, continued gaily down my alley.

"Zero zero" said my scorekeeper, while his disgusted colleague handed me my second shotgun. "Phooey," said the policemen.

Another bird flushed. It angled off through the trees, getting no closer. I took a quick shot with speed inherited from a boyhood spent snap-shooting at woodcock in Maine alder swamps; the pheasant crumpled.

"Hen," shouted my scorekeeper. "Score, zero zero zero." The three policemen made sounds of derision.

Three shots, I said to myself. Score: zero zero zero; seven hundred and ninety-seven shells to go. From far off to the right a bird flushed from the number one lane. Several enthusiasts fired at it without effect. Unmistakably a cock, the bird crossed seventy feet overhead, destination apparently Bratislava. I took a long swing and a long lead, and fired the left barrel. The pheasant struck the ground at our feet.

"*Na zdar!*" cried my retainers—meaning, good going! "Lucky shot," declared the three policemen.

Four shots, score one, seven hundred and ninety-six shots to go, if we used up all our ammunition. Two minutes had passed since we entered the forest.

So it went for those first two miles. The beaters picked up the birds; the hunters touched only their shotguns; and my retainers shouted "Hen, don't shoot!" at suitable moments. With the first fifty shells I killed nineteen pheasants. Both guns grew warm and so did I in my Austrian rompers.

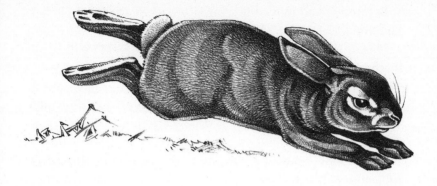

The three members of the Secret Police, treading heavily on the heels of my retainers, continued to make remarks and offer unsolicited observations.

A rabbit finally fixed my policemen. A driven pheasant, with three hundred beaters strung out across the woods, will take off ahead of the marchers. So will foxes and deer, and so—we hoped—would boars disturbed in their slumbers among the acorns. But hares and rabbits combine fright with imagination. A startled rabbit is likely to whip around a stump in a scuffle of leaves and head back toward the line of marchers at forty miles an hour, ears laid flat and hind legs going like pistons. Having failed to kick bunny in the face as he tears by, protocol demands that the hunter continue his dignified advance, facing forward, ignoring the incident. When the line paused presently, I had my opportunity. A hare reversed himself and tore straight at me, eyes wild with apprehension. It dashed between my legs, did a terrified tango through my three faithful retainers, and began broken-field running through the policemen. I spun around one hundred and eighty degrees in the most conspicuously prohibited manner, and deliberately let off a charge of number six shot safely above bunny's head, halfway between two of the policemen. The policemen were not far apart. All three of them went flat on their faces in the yielding Moravian mud. Bunny lengthened his stride.

"Na zdar!" cried my retainers—meaning, good going! "Help!" gurgled the stricken policemen.

I earned a fine symmetrical raspberry from the chief forester, with an assist from the Czech Foreign Office representative. The members of the Secret Police thereafter maintained a prudent and respectful distance to the rear, and they offered no further suggestions regarding my shooting.

There are three different ways to shoot pheasants at Zidlochovice. The first is to flush the birds ahead of the beaters, as we had been doing. Not a difficult shot, with the reservation that a pheasant, tail and rump toward you, can carry away a great many pellets.

The second way is to shoot pheasants head on, from stands, which we did at the end of our trek through the forest. A few hundred yards from the edge of the woods the line of march stopped, and the hunters were led around the outside and took positions facing the woods, at stands in an open field opposite the ten lanes we'd been following. Crowded into the woods we had left was the entire game population that had been moving ahead of us, only now the pheasants were between us and the beaters, who in response to the forester's trumpet resumed their forward movement.

At the edge of the woods, pheasants took wing by the hundred. For fifteen minutes, or until the beaters themselves reached the edge of the woods facing the hunters, everyone fired as fast as his two guns could be passed back and forth between hunter and loader. I killed thirty-eight cock pheasants in a quarter of an hour, and all down the line it sounded like a dress rehearsal for Austerlitz.

The third kind of shooting is High Birds, and that is something else again. The hunters are spaced down the middle of a wide cornfield that separates two tall stands of oaks, mature trees with little undergrowth. The beaters start work half a mile away and each flushed pheasant takes altitude, clears the trees, and then makes off for the forest on the far side of the cornfield. Thus stimulated, with clear air ahead of them, birds fly at sixty to one hundred feet, with the throttle wide open. It takes a lead of eight feet to connect at that distance—more on the quartering angles. Moreover, unless you center your bird, it scales down into the far woods, breakfast for an alert fox, while the score-keeper marks down a succession of zeros. Only pass shooting for geese with the wind behind them is more difficult shooting. My production curve took a downward trend, and I thought respectful thoughts of Carol of Rumania.

At one o'clock we paused for an alfresco luncheon served in a grove of Austrian pines, with *slivovitz* out of little crested glasses and a display of the Hapsburg linen. Waiters recruited from Lippert's in Prague poured steaming goulash into Karlovy Vary soup plates, and there was sharp red wine from nearby Moravian vineyards. I replenished the *slivovitz,* and felt less uncharitable toward my chastened policemen. My shoulder began to stiffen, and in the afternoon I called my own shots and avoided improbable targets.

All afternoon we cruised back and forth between the fields and the forests, and as the shadows lengthened and the sky purpled in the west we came at last to an open space where our three barouches waited, together with wagons filled with all our pheasants and hares and rabbits. The game was unloaded from the wagons by the foresters, who carefully arranged them on the ground in rows, two pheasants at a time, with the hares and rabbits separate from the pheasants. With their plumage of gold and green, the birds made a noble display. The hunters and beaters and foresters faced the hollow square where the game lay, and everyone came to attention. This was the final ceremony of the day, without which no Hapsburg hunt is completed.

The chief forester made a formal speech. He thanked the game for their cooperation, and apologized if they'd been put to any inconvenience. He thanked the hunters for their participation, and he promised additional sport for the morrow. He was like a priest of old time, performing a remembered ritual. I noticed that the Secret Police took no part in the ceremony. Taps was sounded over the field of game, and as the twilight deepened we drove away in our barouches, back to the lodge at Zidlochovice.

On that shoot, ten hunters in a day and a half killed one thousand four hundred and fifty pheasants, and in addition we shot seven hundred hares and three hundred rabbits. Since several of my colleagues developed mashed middle fingers behind the trigger guard, or lacerated jaws and shoulders, fanatics such as the American ambassador made up the difference. I fired upwards of six hundred shells, which I took to represent considerable shooting until I consulted the record. King Carol aforesaid, shooting three double-barreled guns and with an extra bearer and loader, killed eight hundred and thirty-three pheasants during a single day at Zidlochovice. At the most optimistic estimate of his prowess he must have fired over twelve hundred cartridges between eight o'clock in the morning and sunset. The condition of the royal shoulder was not recorded by the local historian, nor—unfortunately—was the effect thereof on Magda Lupescu.

At Zidlochovice the game does not belong to the hunters. It belongs to the Peoples Republic of Czechoslovakia. Communist propaganda about serving pheasants to factory workers in the benign era of the socialist millenium to the contrary notwithstanding, most of the game was shipped with all speed to Western Europe and there swapped for hard currency wherewith to help meet Czechoslovakia's commitments to the Kremlin. A few however were sold to the diplomats who after having tipped the staff at the Zidlochovice Lodge, and subscribed to a present for the chief forester, and paid off the retainers, found they had a fairly substantial investment in harvesting Zapotocky's pheasants. The hunter's privilege of buying game was furthermore conditioned by rank; and an ambassador, as I recall, had access to ten brace, plus five hares and one rabbit, at approximately their cost on the Paris market.

On the road back to Prague the Secret Police finally paid off their accumulated frustration. I drove to the capital after dark, and the Secret Police followed in their black Tatra, fifty feet behind me all the way to the height of land overlooking the Vltava River, blinking their headlights through my rear window. For a hundred and fifty miles they made our life miserable. The embassy attaché who accompanied me wanted to do something about it—borrow the Argentine consul general's revolver, for example. I restrained him. Until we got back to Prague, I said, the slogan remained: Shotguns only!

Pheasants, Vice Admirals, and Lohengrin in Korea

TRADITION HAS it that the ringnecked pheasant origi-
nated in Korea. The bird spread, so the tale goes, from Korea
to Manchuria and from Manchuria south, across the great
rivers to all China. That was centuries ago, even before

Genghis Khan laid siege to Kungwha and, set back on his heels, turned west to conquer the rest of Asia—minus Korea.

Notwithstanding invasions the pheasants prospered, until in the twentieth century one million GIs passed through Korea. When the GIs weren't fighting Communists they spent their spare time chasing pheasants, up and around the sharp eroded hills that overlook the rice paddies. The Korean pheasant population declined to a point that Genghis Khan would have approved of, if pheasants had been Koreans, and the surviving pheasants became sophisticated and wary. That was the situation as I found it, long after the Mongol invasion, while Genghis Khan's unlaundered descendants camped across the Yalu River, glowering.

I reached Korea aboard the old *Bataan*—the C-54 that General MacArthur used when he made good his declaration "I shall return," meaning Manila. We lit down in the *Bataan* in dull November light that darkened the uniforms of the Honor Guard assembled to welcome the new American ambassador. It was one hour to the temporary embassy residence that perched in a fold of the hills overlooking Pusan Harbor, with refugee huts pressing against the walls of our compound. The welcoming martinis had onions at the bottom of their cups and in the shaker the ice had been a long time melting.

The next morning as I started to establish myself in a drafty room in the wartime capital, with rainswept windows grimed by Pusan soot and an eyelashed sprite cheerfully beating the ambassadorial typewriter, I was waited upon by two American admirals. My first visitors were no ordinary American sailors; they were shotgun-shooting, pheasant-hunting, three-star admirals, in full regalia. The day before, while the tired *Bataan* coasted into Korea with flaps pressed down for a gusty landing, the U.S.S. *Missouri* was churning the Strait of Tsushima.

The nearest Communists were north of the thirty-eighth

parallel, unprofitably engaged with the Eighth United States Army, the Fifth Air Force, the First Marine Division, and the Seventh Fleet, so I asked the admirals what else there might be, smaller than the targets off Wonsan the *Missouri* had been lobbing sixteen-inch shells at, over her slanting decks where World War II ended.

"Pheasants," declared the Admirals. "And wild swans, sir," said a voice in the background.

They were three-star admirals, so it was sound ornithology. My own shotguns, coated with grease, were still thousands of miles to the eastward. I borrowed a Browning over-and-under gun from my ranking visitor, a presentation piece with a gold canvasback on one side of the breech and a gold woodcock on the other. The admiral said he had a sound Parker with thirty-inch barrels that had seen him from midshipman at Annapolis to Guantánamo and Coca Sola, and from there to the duckponds east of the Sea of Marmora; he would use the Parker while the ambassador tried out his Browning.

So the next morning off we went, two vice admirals and the new ambassador to Korea, chasing pheasants—plus a voice that had said, "And wild swans, sir."

My wife opened an uneager eye against my predawn departure. She reminded me that a cultural visitor from the Metropolitan Opera was expected to arrive in Pusan that day, with a concert for American soldiers in the evening. The concert, said my wife, had scheduled ambassadorial attendance. I responded with the false heartiness of the hunting husband, and I slid down the hill past the tiny glimmers marking refugee huts to Pusan Pier One, where the two admirals waited.

From a moored LST a commander led a black-and-white setter; she whimpered and put a moist nose in my palm. The commander spoke to the admirals and said something about wild swans. I noticed he carried a carbine instead of a shot-

gun. There was coffee as we settled back in gray Navy sedans, and we headed for the hills that shoulder the Naktong River into the Pusan ricebowl. The admiral's Browning was between my feet, and Miss Mo, the commander's setter, shivered and gave off a strong smell of *kimchi*.

If there is any rougher work in the world than chasing Korean pheasants, it includes dredging Culebra Cut with a handshovel and paddling an overloaded eighteen-foot canoe up Grand Lake in Washington County, Maine, against a northeast wind. The steep Korean hillsides, whereon rain falls each July in torrents, are gravelly and full of treacherous washouts, with brush and vines that catch your ankles. There are loose stones in abundance. One leg becomes shorter than the other in a matter of minutes, and both legs develop muscular twitches. A flushed pheasant enjoys an actuarial advantage it would take a mathematics professor several seconds to compute, before which the pheasant would be over the hill, on his way to the province of Cholla Namdo.

Thus handicapped I added little luster to the admiral's Browning, and my first shot ought to have been my last one. A bright, beautiful cock exploded out of a narrow gully, feet tucked up, white collar gleaming, and his long tail feathers carving the angle of departure. The bird caught both admirals skidding on loose geology in a scuffle of pebbles and profanity. The setter, Miss Mo, and the commander—the latter still carrying his carbine—showed their tonsils in enthusiastic but unhelpful admiration as the pheasant sailed over them.

From where I teetered on a flat stone it was a long downhill shot, and the following *thump* on the bare rice paddy below was the most satisfying sound in the world. Miss Mo gave an incredulous yelp and dashed down the hill, to reappear presently with her head held high and the feet of the bird scuffing the leaves. It was a four-pound cock pheasant, copper and gold and white and green in the sunshine, with a sharp half-inch spur on each ankle, and barred tail feathers over two feet long. The admirals picked themselves up, dusting their pants, and I had the tact to remark that it was the luckiest shot since I left Czechoslovakia. Korea, I decided, was going to be a profitable assignment.

Thereafter, the admirals took over. It was a far bird that got ahead of the senior admiral's Parker. And the junior admiral, who flew an ensign's airplane in World War I long before he put the three-starred flag of the commander of the Seventh Fleet on the U.S.S. *Missouri*, threw number six pellets farther than I could see the targets. As the November haze burned off, the pheasants climbed higher, farther above the rice paddies, and took refuge in inaccessible gullies. It was hot work, and Miss Mo took a progressively more pessimistic view of the prospects. By two o'clock we were exhausted—and famished.

We had sandwiches with thick slabs of rich Uruguayan corned beef off the *Missouri,* and tired hardboiled eggs off the LST, via the commander, who explained that his setter was named not for the battleship but for Miss Mo, the Korean poetess. The junior vice admiral, burrowing into a hamper and politely recalling my first shot, produced a square-shouldered bottle of Jack Daniels, straight from a private cache in Yokosuka.

In any latitude Tennessee sour mash begets beatific contemplation through which I remembered, albeit vaguely, observations of my wife in the Pusan dawn—something about an impending guest from the Metropolitan Opera and a concert that evening for the soldiers; nothing, I concluded, that my wife couldn't cope with better than I could.

The hillside was warm at our backs; the pile of sandwiches diminished and so did the Jack Daniels. We had seven pheasants among us, and the broad Naktong valley spread out to the southward. In the foreground the tiers of rice paddies slanted into ancient canals and the canals in turn to estuaries, until the brown of the harvested fields merged with the blue of farther distances. There were sharp peaks against the horizon; they belonged to the offshore island of Koje, where eighty thousand prisoners of war milled around in their barbed-wire enclosures, hoping for successful armistice negotiations. Seaward, at the mouth of the river, was a broad lagoon, fed by the estuaries.

And presently, across the blue bowl of the afternoon sky, a faraway sound came to us, deep and unmistakable, once heard not readily forgotten—a booming and resonant trumpeting. We looked seaward, and away at the edge of the horizon something white, like distant mirrors, reflected a movement.

"Wild swans," declared the commander.

The trumpeting was renewed, louder and clearer, and the reflected light took processional form in the sky.

"Wild swans," repeated the commander. "They come down from Siberia when the ground freezes. They stay here all winter. Daytime they feed out to sea but in the late afternoon they fly back to the lagoon at the mouth of the river."

The great birds were clearly visible now, circling, gliding down against the wind, presently landing.

"How long," asked the senior admiral, "will it take us to get to the lagoon?"

We fed the last sandwich to Miss Mo and slid down a long escarpment full of loose rocks and stunted pines, collecting one more pheasant and a miscellany of additional bruises and contusions, and we came in the late afternoon to the sloping sea wall that separates the lagoon from the bay between Pusan and Chinhae.

The commander had out a box of heavy shells, BB shot with three and three-quarters drams of powder per cartridge, which he divided among us.

"Sirs," said the commander, "the idea is for you three to spread out along the sea wall and hide behind it, while I crawl around the west side of the lagoon and stir them up with the rifle. They'll probably be out of range but I'll put them up for you. When the swans flush, they'll head out to sea again, right over you. They may be high," he concluded.

"Son," said one of the admirals, "have you ever done this before?"

"Six times, sir," said the commander.

"And did you ever get one of those swans?"

"No, sir," admitted the commander.

The commander and Miss Mo disappeared about their business, which I gathered was likely to be aquatic. The admirals and I crawled over the sea wall about one hundred yards apart and poked our heads cautiously in the direction of the lagoon. There were the swans, half a mile away, two hundred of the noblest birds in the world. They looked like toy sailboats in the Luxembourg Garden—or real sailboats halfway across Long Island Sound. The sun dipped behind the Chinhae hills, darkening the west side of the lagoon, where the commander and Miss Mo, not visible to us, were probably wading and crouching. The temperature dropped and as evening came on I again remembered our operatic guest and her concert in Pusan.

We saw the swans move before we heard the commander's shot. At that distance it was first a confused disturbance on the water followed by the crack of his carbine and the beat of great wings lifted together, and then clear and fine over the lagoon the trumpet call of the birds as they settled into the pattern of formation flying.

The swans passed directly over us, precisely as the commander predicted. It was the finest sight since flamingos over Lake Junín at thirteen thousand feet in an Andean sunrise. The swans were clear against the darkening sky, long neck distended, still climbing with every wingbeat.

The two admirals and I emptied our shotguns, and with the commander's overloaded ammunition the jolt made my teeth rattle. I fired the second barrel leaning backward, twenty feet ahead of the lead bird of three, and the kick knocked me into the shallow water at the foot of the sea wall.

No swan hesitated or lost a wingbeat, and no feather came drifting down. Serene in their evening sky, trumpeting defiantly, the great raft of white birds moved majestically out to sea. They were so large they looked like bombers, power full on, come up from the end of a runway.

The admirals and I climbed disgustedly from our concealment and started walking toward the Navy sedans parked beyond the sea wall. "Those birds must have been five hundred feet over our heads," declared the senior admiral. "What we needed was an anti-aircraft battery off the *Missouri*. Hell with that kind of shooting."

We climbed aboard the sedan to wait for the commander, and the junior admiral resurrected the Jack Daniels.

Our first sight of our commander, half and hour later, was down the road by the sea wall, sharp in the Chevrolet headlights. He looked like an advertisement for Scott's Emulsion, complete with burden, leaning forward into the weight over his shoulder. The swan's head and reddish black beak hung below the commander's waist, and the long white neck was thick as an upholstered firehose. Miss Mo, trotting at the commander's side with plumed tail waving, was obviously ready to claim at least half of the credit.

"Son," said the senior vice admiral, "if I put this on your report, it'd make me out a liar. I don't believe it."

"Sir," said the commander, off-loading twenty-seven pounds of wild swan and shucking the cartridges out of his carbine, "my bullet ricocheted. The birds were way out of range. I mean the bullet keyholed, sir, like a flat stone over the water. The bullet was side-on when it hit. Knocked him cold. Really, sir, I mean it. He was upside down when we got there in a sampan."

From the junior vice admiral came a sound dominated by Tennessee sour mash, and then he offered the bottle to the commander. "My boy," he said, "you give that damn swan to the American ambassador. Nobody else would believe you."

On the way back to Pusan we deposited the senior admiral at K-1 airport where his plane waited to return him to his Tokyo headquarters; it seemed a long time since I'd landed there in General MacArthur's *Bataan* just two days earlier. Later, back at Pier One in Pusan, we said good-by to the commander of the Seventh Fleet while respectful naval ratings manned his barge and the U.S.S. *Missouri* lay four miles out, beyond the breakwater. Both admirals took pheasants, minus the cock bird which dedicated my Korean shooting, but both admirals insisted—with the commander and Miss Mo helping to out-vote me—that the wild swan belonged to the new American ambassador.

Our house still perched on the hillside overlooking Pusan harbor, with refugee huts crowding the walls of the compound. It was nearly ten o'clock at night, and whatever my wife had achieved for patriotic music must long since have been accomplished. Our first house guest, I remembered, had come to Korea to bring song to expatriate GIs. The heartiness of my predawn departure evaporated in an end-of-day feeling that my long defection was possibly reprehensible.

I lifted the swan from the back of the Navy sedan and held him up in the light from the doorway. That was the largest bird I'd seen since a mounted condor in the Lima museum, displayed beside a life-size statue of Atahualpa, the last of the Incas.

My wife appeared in the doorway, with the smile of the wife of a husband who goes hunting. Beside her was a large and very impressive lady. "Did you have a good day?" asked my wife. And then, "But I thought you and your admirals were out chasing pheasants."

Our guest from the Metropolitan examined the tremendous white bird that measured eight feet from wingtip to wingtip. The black webbed feet were as big as the rubber flippers frogmen wear when they go spear-fishing.

"*Si eso es un faisán,*" she declared in a voice husky from singing to fifteen hundred American GIs at Pusan head-quarters, "*entonces soy yo Lily Pons, o quizás Helen Trau-bel.*" Which was to say that if that bird was a pheasant, she herself was two other people. She admired the commander's swan, and I felt my spirits coming up. In rusty Spanish I explained how the commander had shot it. "*Un tiro bastante largo,*" I said, "*a través de la laguna.*"

"I'll bet it was," said our guest in a good midwest American accent. "But you come home late, Mr. Ambassador. With a swan like that, two hours ago, I could have given your soldiers *Lohengrin*—and made them like it."

The Pheasants of Cheju Island

WE WERE in Seoul, the war-scarred capital of Korea, planning our hunting. "Trouble with this assignment, Horace," I said, "is that when you and your cameras get lined up so a pheasant is in range, and the light and the focus are right, then either there won't be any ringneck in that Korean buckwheat patch, or else the volcanic wall will collapse and leave you flat on your fanny when you ought to be earning your living by taking a picture."

This abrasive but prophetic remark was aimed at Horace Bristol, *Life* photographer in the Far East, whose pictures of the Korean War are classics. When *Sports Illustrated* suggested I do a piece for them on pheasant hunting, to have Horace Bristol participate was an extra dividend of distinction. Horace had the workout of his career, which I possibly shortened.

The best pheasant shooting is on Cheju Island—Cheju-do, our Korean friends call it—and thither we repaired, Horace with a festoon of professional cameras and I with a twenty-gauge Winchester Model 21—for pheasants, the weapon of an incurable optimist. A borrowed pointer accompanied us; he proved a millstone of some weight around the neck of the hunters.

Where the Yellow Sea meets the Straits of Tsushima and the mustard-colored water turns jade over the deep, there lies Cheju-do. Hallasan, the volcanic peak of the island, rises ten feet higher than Mount Washington in New Hampshire. From there the view extends fifty miles to the Korean mainland and twice as far in the opposite direction to Kyushu in Japan, where the fishermen keep an eye peeled for Syngman Rhee's coast guard.

Centuries ago Cheju-do was a matriarchate and the only males on the premises except boys and patriarchs were seasonal utilitarians, present by invitation. Between times the ladies of Cheju-do made a bare living by diving in thirty feet of cold water for abalone, which they exchanged with the mainland for rice and layettes. They also grubbed up handfuls of edible seaweed—dulse we call it around Passamoquoddy and the Bay of Fundy—and their bathing suits were abbreviated. This custom interested the GIs chaperoning Chinese

Communist prisoners of war on Cheju-do, hundreds of years later.

Kublai Khan visited Cheju-do. He found no sites comparable to Xanadu for a pleasure dome but instead established a horse farm. To this day the Cheju-do ponies have the hammer heads and strong chests that carried the Mongol warriors across all of Asia, clear to the Danube River. Kublai's son once demanded two thousand Cheju-do horses from his Korean cousin, who forthwith invaded the island to find out what went on there. The ladies prudently retreated up the mountain, but from Hallasan they rolled rocks down the hillside until the bruised Korean king went back and reported that the derby pickings weren't worth Ming dynasty bourbon. That ended Kublai's horse-breeding project.

A Dutchman took the first European look at Cheju-do, in 1653, when Captain Hendrik Hamel, an articulate philosopher already bent by a lost horizon, went aground there in a storm. His initial response was optimistic. "Six of us," Captain Hamel wrote, "were allowed to go Ashore by Turns, to take the Air and wash our Linnens." The Ladies Aid thereupon did so well by the shipwrecked mariners that it took the skipper fourteen years to get back from Cheju-do to Holland with his manuscript. Captain Hamel also noted, "There are many birds on the Island. They are called Fezants, and they are very Cunning."

In World War II, Cheju-do was an important Japanese base, guarding the entrance to the Eastern Sea. When American bombers interested themselves in the place, the Japanese dug caves on the cone of Hallasan and thereafter, in the Korean War, those high retreats became convenient shelters for guerillas who so successfully defied the authorities that when General Mark Clark and I visited Cheju-do in 1953 to verify Captain Hamel's ornithology, each pheasant hunter was accompanied by an MP armed with a carbine. The idea was that if General Clark or I flushed a pheasant, that was what we were there for; but if instead we flushed a Communist guerilla, an MP with his carbine was supposed to take over.

Having an MP on your heels with his rifle at half-cock stimulates perception, but the only people we met on the Hallasan uplands were American Marines, hunting deer without benefit of bodyguards. The Marines admired our four-star jeep and wished us Good Hunting. We shot thirty pheasants.

I returned to Cheju-do the following year, after the Korean Armistice, with Horace Bristol, the photographer, and Lo Hung Sam, the borrowed mongrel pointer. We lit down in a tired C-47 on a grass field, two hours from Seoul, and went immediately to work in the November sunshine. Conditions, said Horace, were excellent for photography. Lo Hung Sam sniffed what we hoped was pheasant-laden air, and he seemed to take an equally cheerful view of the prospects.

And work it is, hunting pheasants on Cheju Island. If a profligate Congress paid ambassadors by the ton-mile instead of by the year, the American taxpayers would take a beating every time an ambassador goes hunting. What topnotch photographers are paid is unreported—doubtless more than diplomats, and they are probably worth it; but that week end Horace earned every dime he collected. In addition to Halla-san, which hasn't erupted since the year 1007, the island fathered a large family of lesser volcanos, which look from the air like cups with chipped rims, scattered at random over the hillsides. Out of each cup, aeons ago, poured jagged rocks of every dimension. They bounded down in a torrent of angry rubble, and across the succeeding centuries the Cheju-do lady farmers sorted them out with housewifely care, building stone walls to enclose their tiny patches of farmland. The soil is not fertile, but for miles from the sea-shore these brown walls are continuous, with each separate plot rarely covering more than one acre.

Above the farms, whence the view north across the ocean fades to the blue profile of the Korean mainland, there are sloping uplands with fewer stone walls but with a grass cover so heavy and so interlaced with green vines that progress afoot is as hard as slogging through knee-deep snow. This is Kublai Khan's horse country, largely abandoned today because of guerillas. The pheasants take to these uplands in winter, after the coastal crops are harvested by the hard-working Cheju-do women.

In the low country where we hunted, the farmers cultivate millet and buckwheat with patches of sweet potato, corn, and red peppers. The women rake out each spring additional rocks for their walls, which are made without mortar or adobe—just loose stones, carefully selected and laboriously fitted together. Their walls are two or three feet wide at the base, tapering to a thin upper edge topped with stones no larger than your fist. Chest high around most of the fields, the walls at some places reach ten or twelve feet.

All Cheju-do walls have one characteristic in common: they are excessively collapsible. Lean against one, and yards of rock tilt outward and disintegrate. There follows a rumble of stones grinding together, and then comes a cloud of brown volcanic dust from the center of which the bruised hunter picks himself up, wounded in body and spirit, hoping his shotgun isn't irretrievably damaged.

The way for the hunter to cross a Cheju-do stone wall is to knock down enough of it so he can step across, which is a difficult maneuver because the far side is then littered with loose stones, treacherously tilted. Or else he crawls across, which is even more difficult because the large lower rocks are sharp-edged as meteorites, and imperfectly balanced.

Pecking away at the grain within these enclosed fields there are, as Captain Hamel reported, "many birds called Fezants, and they are very Cunning."

Although shotguns on Cheju-do are a recent menace to

bird life, the local ringnecks quickly learned to associate the sound of a collapsing wall with an approaching hunter, timing their take-offs accordingly. This astuteness paid off, for otherwise the pheasants would have had a rough time with American soldiers whose work guarding Communist prisoners of war in stockades on the island still left them opportunities for plenty of bird shooting. The stone walls constituted a further protection; there are few experiences more frustrating to a hunter than straddling one of those walls, with a sixty-pound rock poised over your ankle, when a cock pheasant with tail feathers two feet long rises within easy range and then goes soaring to safety.

The Cheju-do farmers tolerate the damage by hunters to their masonry because pheasants have a voracious appetite for the same grains they so diligently cultivate against the hunger of winter. That much we learned from an aged citizen in a long white robe whom we found taking his ease behind a corn shock, smoking a pipe with a tiny brass bowl and a lengthy bamboo stem. In his other hand he held what appeared to be a very large cigar, tied around with a string. Since two-handed smokers are rare in my frugal New England, I inquired of the patriarch, "How come?" The cigar, replied the ancient, was slow-burning punk, the all-day fuse for his pipe-smoking achievement—his Cheju-do box of matches. I contributed a Manila *blunt*—a lethal gift to the uninitiated—which the patriarch immediately lighted from the end of his fuse. He declared, between coughs, that it was all right for us to go on knocking down his stone walls; the women would repair them tomorrow. We left him contentedly mingling Philippine tobacco smoke with the aroma of *kimchi*.

It was a clear November afternoon and in no time Horace was clicking his shutters like castanets and loping back and forth behind our wall-crumbling line of march, covering nearly as much ground as our borrowed pointer, whom Horace spotted forty-seven years, not to forget a second pair of legs that proved to be just the thing for vaulting stone walls with. Lo Hung Sam was black, enthusiastic, and idiotic —an unhelpful combination.

There were plenty of pheasants, and presently I knocked one down, at which point it became evident that Sam was a blessing as mixed as his ancestry. Sam was fine at trailing a wounded bird, but unless the hunter was close behind— which was difficult because of the stone walls—Sam's quarry was likely to be overzealously mangled before being surrendered. And since disabled pheasants invariably fell in a field beyond the hunter, pursuit was an undertaking marked by rockfalls, contusions, and unfriendly observations about Lo Hung Sam's alleged pointer grandmother. Sam demolished a pheasant before Horace could say "Leica," and when Sam did so, the game was in no condition to interest an illustrated weekly.

Chastised and admonished, Sam eventually found a perfect point. That is, it was a point as perfect as his slightly bent tail and low-hung chassis would accommodate, and I hopefully closed in, with quickening pulses. My gun was poised and my hopes high. But out of the millet, sudden as a firecracker, popped a terrified Korean rabbit. Sam broke point with a yelp of pure joy. Together, dog and rabbit, they cleared the nearest stone wall like guided missiles in flat trajectory.

When Sam tardily reappeared, minus the rabbit, Horace was sympathetic. He said he already had over two hundred pictures, and he added that his pants were torn in conspicuous places. Horace suggested we call it a day. "Let's try tomorrow for sunrise pictures," said Horace, "—pictures in color."

On the morrow I got my first double of the 1954 season. A double in pheasants, and with a twenty-gauge at that, is an event not lightly to be recounted. We had coffee in a deserted

Army mess, a sleepy but amiable sergeant officiating, and by dawn we were back on the flank of Hallasan, tall tufted grass waving in the chill breeze of approaching day, while the eastern sky turned from purple to crimson. Lo Hung Sam did not witness that Cheju-do sunrise. Sam was chained to the door of the sergeant's doghouse, happily dreaming of rabbits.

The excellence of Horace's photographs is proverbial. But one photograph will nevertheless be conspicuously missing.

We had crossed innumerable stone walls, with the industrious little Cheju-do women rallying in our wake to put back the stones almost as fast as we dislodged them, when we came to a patch of buckwheat that looked especially promising. I was on the inside of the wall, by dint of precarious climbing, and Horace was on the far side, looking for an opening. While he searched for it, my naval attaché and I deployed to the far end of the patch and walked slowly back, scuffing the pink buckwheat stems that had ripe white heads on them. There presently remained only a sparse crescent of grass against the wall Horace had by this time gallantly mounted. The Korean sun was warm on our shoulders; the light was good; the view was clear. All the portents had finally reached symmetrical conjunction.

As we entered the grass, up went three pheasants from that improbable concealment. They were a noble sight—two hens and a big cock—three pheasants against the Cheju-do morning sky, bodies angled upward, gaining altitude with every wingbeat. My naval attaché folded one hen at the moment I centered the other. Then he generously lowered his Parker while I polished off the cock twenty feet in front of the ace photographer of Asia. Three birds down—two a double; my first double of the season. The unforgettable moment. Like Lo Hung Sam in sight of his rabbit, I yelped with joy and surged forward. The moment of triumph—photographed by Horace in indelible color. . . .

It was a victorious but brittle moment, shattered by the sound behind me. That sound was made by a stone wall collapsing. There was a rumble of ancient rocks grinding together, and there followed the rattle of small stones cascading after. A mushroom of brown volcanic dust momentarily obscured the details. The cloud spread, hung briefly in the air, and then shredded away on the winds of the morning. Horace was disclosed bottom side up among the rocks, festooned with his battered equipment.

We helped Horace to his feet, while he tested his reflexes. With a silk handkerchief he carefully removed the volcanic dust from his lenses and examined his three cameras with professional attention, whereafter he applied the same handkerchief to his bleeding knuckles. He gingerly rubbed his shin and contemplated an irreparable rent in his trousers.

"You'd better go pick up your birds," Horace observed mildly. "That was fine shooting. Unfortunately I missed it. And from now on, Mr. Ambassador, you and Kublai Khan and Lo Hung Sam can do this and that with all the pheasants in Korea."

A Helicopter Is a Duck's Best Friend

SHOOTING GAME birds from a helicopter has been de-
nounced by conservationists as a wicked enterprise engaged
in—contrary to good citizenship—by the same adults who
when adolescent probably snipped the wings off sparrows

with grandmother's sewing scissors. No true sportsman, reads this legend, would have any part in the slaughter of our defenseless Feathered Friends, mowed down by a man in a helicopter, shooting a shotgun.

A purpose of these observations is to record that people who think shooting by helicopter puts a hex on Old Mother Nature need to have their heads examined. I'm not talking about the big new contraptions that carry a platoon of soldiers plus an amphibious jeep; conceivably if you mounted an atomic cannon on the bow you might now and then collect a handful of feathers. What I'm describing is the plexiglas-bubble helicopter manufactured by an articulate tribesman named Bell, who when the Korean war broke out shipped his choppers to the stricken peninsula with the result, among others, that there are hundreds of GIs alive today whose bones would otherwise be crumbling in the United Nations cemetery outside Pusan.

On the left side of the bubble sits a first lieutenant of Marines. He attends strictly to business because the pilot of a chopper has to fly it every second, with no strolling aft for a quick cup of coffee with the stewardess. In fact there is no aft, except a skeletal fuselage with a small propeller at the far end. This prop is brightly painted so pedestrians won't be conked by it while the helicopter is idling. It takes up the torque generated by the rotor blades. Otherwise the bubble would spin around and around like a top, and chopper pilots would get even dizzier than they do anyway.

A helicopter pilot is selected by ground exercises during which he proves he can simultaneously pat his head, rub his stomach, and play "Barcarole" on the church organ with either foot. This is the sort of extrasensory three-dimensional coordination that shortly gets the card of a candidate into an IBM machine—one card among hundreds—from which presently out pops a chopper pilot, bound for the First Marine Division in Korea.

Underneath the plexiglass bubble are two round metal skis that do duty as landing gear and, when the chopper is on official business, as supports for a pair of stretchers, each with room for a wounded soldier in a canvas container. In those days the helicopters served the front lines, shuttling between there and the afterdeck of the Danish hospital ship *Jutlandia,* anchored off Inchon. By helicopter a casualty was often on the operating table within an hour of his wound, and is up and about today, bragging about it. Or so they tell it around the First Marine Division, where chopper pilots are honored among men and can do no wrong, not even on Saturdays following pay day.

Our helicopter expedition had nothing to do with casualties but was replete with scientific interest. There had come a lull in the Korean winter fighting and the general invited me to help him test a new cold-weather uniform, just received in the theater. Mallard ducks were to be incidental to the testing. So I came to Seoul from our temporary embassy in Pusan, and at Eighth Army Headquarters the general presented me with a Cold Bar suit, the latest example of the genius of the quartermaster's establishment.

The Cold Bar suit, which I took to be army idiom for a garment designed to bar cold, was made of foam rubber and plastic. It was in the shape of long-handled winter underwear, stretching from wrists to ankles. This garment was worn next the skin, tight all over. I discarded my wool hunting clothes and wriggled into the Cold Bar suit the way a plump debutante gets into her girdle. I looked around for the rest of the costume. Mickey Mouse boots and a knitted cap completed the picture. That was all there was to it. The effect, with a hunter inside, was vaguely that of a Michelin tire advertisement.

Cased in rubber, my body immediately became a fireless cooker, which was doubtless the idea of the scientists assisting the quartermaster. Against the contingency of overheating, the suit had a series of vents, fore and aft, worked by zippers.

"If you get too hot," said the general, "just pull on a zipper."

I presently tried it, out of doors, and wished I hadn't. The entering air was ten above zero, and on my moist bare skin it felt like scalding ether.

The general explained that our test was to be conducted down the Han River, twenty miles from Seoul, accessible by Marine Corps helicopter. "If there's any colder place this side of the Yalu," said the general, "the ducks won't know it. Just the place to try out a new uniform. Furthermore, we'll get some shots on the way, out of the choppers. Ever flown in a chopper?" I said, Never.

As described, the project was simple. You sat in the plexiglass bubble, with the right door removed, and pretty soon you cruised alongside a handsome mallard. You took the mallard with one neat shot and the chopper darted down like a dragonfly while you retrieved your duck. At destination in the Han valley the two choppers were to deposit the hunters among the ice cakes scattered along the margin of the river. The helicopters would then scout up- and downstream. The mallards would take wing and zoom past the ice cakes. While thus profitably engaged, the hunters would also be testing the effectiveness of the new Cold Bar uniform.

We climbed aboard at the old Seoul racetrack. The lieutenant removed the door on my side and remarked, deferentially, that I looked like a Michelin advertisement. I said the same thought had occurred to me. The pilot also said not to shoot in line with the general's helicopter, and please to be careful with high shots.

I could understand why rattling number four pellets off

the general's plexiglass would be a poor way to cement friendly relations between the State Department and the Army—but why no high shots?

"On account of the blades," said the pilot. "One high shot and you'll make my rotors look like an egg-beater."

I agreed to pass up the ducks on the upper horizon. The lieutenant started his motor. A wind off Manchuria poured into the bubble and clawed at the bag of shotgun shells between my feet. I quickly made sure all the ventilating zippers on the Cold Bar uniform were fastened. The lieutenant loosened my safety belt, shouting in my ear that for accurate shooting you had to lean way out, as far as possible through the open door space. "The general," he yelled, "steps clean out and rests his right foot on the ski. But to do that you've got to wear the belt so loose you're likely to slide through it."

I replied, against the noise that gave that flying machine its nickname of chopper, that I intended to stay inside—well inside—the plexiglass bubble.

It was a gray January day with banked clouds in the north where the MIGs lived, and I hoped we wouldn't see any. The rotor blades spun faster. The lieutenant twirled a ring below the black handle of the control stick and moved the stick forward. The racetrack slowly fell away below us. At two hundred feet we edged into the north wind, over the blasted walls and roofless buildings of the capital of Korea.

Riding a bubble is like peddling a bicycle in the sky. Seoul changed hands four times in the first nine months of fighting. Deducting a few heavy shells contributed by the U.S.S. *Missouri* to soften up the Commies for the Inchon landing, it had all been hand-to-hand, street-by-street encounter—savage, bitter, and destructive. Only Warsaw and Manila saw greater punishment. We sailed over the rubble of the red-and-white post office, pride of Japanese days, past the ruins of Duksoo Palace. Beyond was the American Embassy compound, with the mark of sentries' feet in the fresh snow but no smoke coming from the residence chimney. Next door the Russian Legation was a twisted wreck with little above ground except the white tower, winking emptily at the sky.

Climbing, we cleared the West Gate by fifty feet. The old city wall, built by the first Yi emperor in case the grandchildren of Genghis Khan should come back, followed the crest of hills on either side. Ahead lay the Han River valley, with frozen rice paddies on either side. Tiny villages nestled in the contours, their thatched roofs a series of facing Ls.

I loaded my shotgun. Poking the barrel into the slipstream I could feel the wind pressure and I wondered how our forward speed—eighty miles by the needle—against a thirty-mile wind in the opposite direction would affect the equations of lead and trajectory. The top side of the open doorway was low enough so a high shot—as prohibited by the pilot—would be hard to make without squatting. Since squatting was ruled out by the safety belt, which I had promptly retightened, the lieutenant's rotor blades seemed safe enough. I was comfortably warm in my Cold Bar suit, and I looked for the general. His chopper had prudently taken position on our port side, two hundred yards away, out of range of stray pellets. The general, I could see, was leaning out of it.

Korea is a main flyway for ducks driven by early autumn cold from the marshes of Siberia. Beginning in mid-October, before the Korean rice harvest is over, migratory birds come crowding into the narrow peninsula. First ducks to arrive are the little teal that splash around the fresh-water ponds behind the irrigation dikes. Three weeks later, when the teal have crossed the Yellow Sea to move south along the China coast, come the gray geese and the big green-head mallards —hardy birds that spend all winter on the coast of Korea. They pass their days wherever open water occurs: around the indented coast, at the mouth of the Naktong, and in the valley of the Han north of Seoul, where the great tides from Inchon crack the river ice each day and the jagged cakes churn up the succulent marsh grass. But what the ducks prize above all else is rice, scattered on the paddies during the harvest—thousands and thousands of grains to the acre. In a country of little snow and high winds, this frozen banquet lasts all winter, and Korean mallards are heavily laden. Toward evening the ducks leave open water and crowd noisily into the paddies. Later in my Korean service, when I had learned the rhythm of their habits, I had elegant full-moon shooting on a new snow, while F-86s whooshed overhead from Kimpo, charting weird streaks in the winter sky.

In five minutes from the racetrack we were over the Han River. Almost immediately we saw ducks. Better yet, the ducks were recognizably mallards.

A duck seen from above is a different proposition from the bird you jump ten yards from the silent canoe nosing up a dead-water stream in Maine. Ducks on the water, viewed from above, are gray ovals one second and gray comets the next, flying in every direction like bits of a hand grenade, while the water that is now below them boils with the agitation of their departure.

In theory ducks flushed by a helicopter ought to take off in a group and all fly in the same direction. The pilot would then maneuver in their wake and soon the flock would be overtaken. Because the forward speed of the chopper would not greatly exceed the flying speed of the ducks, shooting them ought to be as easy as gathering pecans in Texas. Thereupon *Ducks Unlimited* would pass an angry resolution. That is, theoretically.

Twenty-five shots later I was still trying to hit my first mallard. They flew downwind and upwind and crosswind, and some of them almost flew into the plexiglass bubble.

I shot downwind and upwind and crosswind, with long leads and small leads and no leads, each shot with mounting frustration. As I tore open my second box of shells I observed the general, with his chopper canted sideways when he put his weight on the right ski, leaning inboard, like a man in a king-size kiddiecar rounding a corner. Puffs of smokeless powder marked the general's progress.

It was a fine thrill and a corresponding surprise when on my twenty-ninth shot I polished off a drake mallard and watched him go end over end to a sand bar two hundred feet below us—as dead a duck as I'd ever picked out of a flock by a Chesapeake blind or a Patagonian pampas. Only trouble was—the duck I'd killed was at least thirty feet away from the mallard I'd aimed at.

The lieutenant followed my duck with his chopper like a plummeting falcon. He landed on the frozen sand and I retrieved the bird. That much, at least, was according to preflight briefing. Downwind, the general's chopper pirouetted behind an ice cake as big as a barn, and I walked over to find out how he was doing. The general had three mallards and one red fox. The fox, he said, was loping along the top of a dike: never even saw him. I remarked that since foxes eat mallards, the balance was thus far on the side of conservation. It was a plump red fox, prime furred, and the brush was admirable.

"This is a good place," said the general, "here where the river bends. We can send the helicopters to beat up and down the river. The choppers will flush the ducks for us."

It was three o'clock and the winter afternoon was bitter. So was the wind where it got around our wrists, but inside the Cold Bar suit our bodies were perspiring against the rubber. Just the uniform, declared the general, for a soldier manning an observation post; maybe even a sentry. He said he was delighted with the experiment; he would so report to Washington. I replied that is was certainly handier than a bulky hunting coat, and what kind of lead did the general take anyway, shooting ducks out of a chopper?

The general's answer was lost in the sound of our departing helicopters. He said we had an hour of shooting, including the time it would take the choppers to refuel at Kimpo. He suggested I find a cake of ice large enough for concealment, while he did the same two hundred feet downriver. He cautioned me against climbing over the ice piled toward midstream, observing that with Mickey Mouse boots on, anyone pulled under the floe by the current was a gone Indian. He strode off, looming large, martial, and competent in his Cold Bar uniform.

The choppers diligently scoured the valley, and there were plenty of mallards. The drawback was that the ducks scattered in all directions ahead of the beaters, and by the time the ranks were re-formed the birds were flying about five hundred feet up, a range that not even the general's magnum could dominate. I blew off the rest of my second box of shells and knocked down one duck that was ten yards behind the bird I was leading. It fell winged, and by the time I got back from chasing it across the ice I was winded and sat down, cautiously, for the ice cakes were not only full of rocks gouged out of the river bank but also prickly with frozen shards and sharp edges. I was sweating, but a tug on a zipper fixed that; the sweat froze almost before I could close the opening, and I wasted no time closing it.

The helicopters left to refill their tanks. With no aerial beaters the ducks settled down. Soon they would be moving out of the river for their supper of rice on the paddies. Far overhead I could hear jets, flying thousands of feet above the gray overcast. I was snug in my elastic cocoon. I thought how useful for Korean winter shooting might be one of those *pappa-san* white coats the local patriarchs wear, and I resolved to get one to camouflage my fine new military equipment.

The sound of mallards penetrated my meditations. A long skein of birds traced the western horizon. Far out of range they swung, turning low against the bare hillside, and approached upwind, following the open channel of the river. Wedged among the tilted blocks of ice, my Cold Bar suit black against the gray, I made myself as inconspicuous as possible. They came on, but the lead drake saw me. He flared and his followers tilted their wings and depressed their tailfeathers, curving upward and away in the wake of their leader. The spread V had been parallel to the river, and the rear guard was accordingly closer along the line of flight than the lead bird. This was the kind of shooting a man could account for. I stood up and took a ten-foot lead on the nearest climbing mallard, shortened it automatically as the bird came on, then poured on the powder. It was a fair target and I centered my mallard. Then they were all out of range, fanning upward toward the overcast.

Downriver the general fired one shot only. This was immediately followed by a yell that reverberated all up and down the Han River valley, blunt and loud and far-reaching.

Halfway to pick up my mallard I was spun around as if by a magnet by the echoes of that yell. That same sound, thirty-four years before, must have lifted his entire company out of a Flanders trench, and got his entire division from Anzio to Rome a quarter-century later. It was a leather-lunged effort, as surprising in that frozen Korean valley as Pat Hurley's Choctaw war whoop must have been at the Teheran Conference. It was followed by other sounds, equally hearty, and those I interpreted, as I shortened the intervening distance among the ice blocks, as mingled suffering and fury. Generals, I told myself, don't have hunting accidents. Handling firearms is second nature to them. And the general hadn't fallen through the ice, or he couldn't be shouting.

When I reached him, the general stood, but he stood not to attention. He was holding both hands against the seat of his trousers, or what would have been the seat of his trousers if he had still been in the uniform exchanged earlier that afternoon for a Cold Bar suit, the quartermaster's latest confection for intemperate weather. Sounds continued to pour from him in a furious torrent.

"Goddam quartermaster," he roared. "Swindling the taxpayers. I'll bust that soanso back to corporal. I knew this pantywaist must have a gimmick. . . ." The general moved, then winced when the cold air struck him. "I was hunkered down between cakes of ice, off balance. Recoil jarred me back. Stone sharp as a damn razor. All the winter weather this side of Manchuria is inside my pants!"

I examined the general's Cold Bar suit. There was indeed a puncture, like a cut automobile tire, at the point indicated, which was where the seat of my host's pants would have been if my host had been wearing his pants. And that aperture had no zipper, so every time the general moved—and he was a moving man—air at ten degrees above zero, with a thirty-knot wind behind it, penetrated his rubber rompers. From my own experiments with the Cold Bar built-in ventilating system, I knew what that air felt like, and I could imagine where it hit him. By standing still, in a post not tailored for generals, some of the frost was kept in the Han River valley. But when he stopped swearing, the general's teeth chattered.

"Got a muffler or a scarf?" he demanded. "No? Neither have I. There isn't even a vest pocket in this goddam girdle. Your cap—no, keep your cap on. Your ears would freeze solid as doorknobs."

It was an unhappy general, standing in the position of him who has recently been paddled. Unquestionably our experiment was reaching a crisis. Remedial measures were becoming not only overdue but imperative.

"Wait a minute," I said. "Stand fast and try not to move." I went away, as fast as the Mickey Mouse boots allowed, and came back with the game. "Diplomacy to the rescue! Frostbite is the mother of invention. . . . Now, if you don't mind bending over, General. Sorry . . . the Duck's head is too small. Hold on! I have it. The foxtail . . ."

"My friend," said the general presently. "Diplomacy is OK. You can quote me. . . ."

Walking, burdened with the body of the fox held behind him, the general and I headed for the sand bar. We proceeded slowly. But the tail just fitted the rent in the general's Cold Bar uniform and, with the general cradling the fox in clasped hands, while I carried the shotguns and the ducks, we got there as our two choppers landed. I offered to cut off the fox's tail but the same lack of pockets that failed to produce a scarf failed also to accommodate a knife, and somehow shooting the tail off the fox didn't seem very sporting. So the general carried the fox—a new version of the fable about the young man of Sparta, a couple of millenniums earlier. I forebore to remind my host of that fable.

The two Marine lieutenants were unprepared for the spectacle of a several-star general, regular Army, wearing a red fox for a bustle. They themselves had on feather-lined flying suits and blue parkas borrowed from the Fifth Air Force. They had consumed hot coffee at Kimpo while their choppers refueled. Mindful of rank, they politely said nothing about the general's unexpected decoration. "How was the shooting?" they asked. "Too bad. Damn jets probably give ducks the jitters."

The general backed into his helicopter, rear first, fox and all, after telling his pilot to unload his shotgun. With that following wind the flight back to Seoul took us fifteen minutes. There were ducks on the way and I aimed at them, but my wand continued as ineffective as a moist Roman candle. When I landed at the racetrack two minutes behind the general, he was already in his heated sedan. It had a red plate and silver stars on it.

The general's pilot brought me the fox. He saluted. "General's compliments, sir. General says tally-ho to you, sir." The sedan drove away and the lieutenant made no further observation. But around First Marine Corps headquarters, and wherever chopper pilots foregathered, I predicted that a startling and spectacular tradition would soon be a-cooking.

The Korean winter waned, and an armistice followed. The general retired from the Army with many years and much merit. Last time I saw him he was complaining that if the Pentagon hadn't held him back he could have marched north, clear to Manchuria, and chased every damn Communist out of Korea. He might have at that. But not by helicopter. And certainly not in a Cold Bar uniform with a fox for a mascot!

Animal Interlude—with Bears

FIRST TIME I saw President Rhee's bears was three months before the Korean Armistice and right after the smaller bear bit the minister of foreign affairs, an agile little man who flew out of his chair like a cork from a bottle, bumping his head on the wisteria arbor and startling the bumblebees, which zoomed around us like angry helicopters, while the minister rubbed his ankle and Captain Kwak, of the presidential guard, dived under the garden table after the cubs, wearing heavy gloves. The larger bear then weighed twenty pounds and his sister, after sampling the foreign minister of Korea, about five pounds less. They were handsome cubs, sleek and roly-poly and black, and each one had a white V-for-Victory mark on his chest.

It was some minutes before we got back to the armistice negotiations because President Rhee went off with Captain Kwak to find out how the bears had escaped from their pen. "The bears come from the mountains near the Eastern Sea," the president explained. "The mother was shot by one of our soldiers, but he caught the two cubs. I am sorry about the bite."

Dr. Pyun, massaging his ankle, politely said it was nothing, and we resumed our consideration of the armistice negotiations taking place at Panmunjom, thirty miles north. The bumblebees settled back into the purple and white wisteria blossoms and the president declared, with vigor, that he wanted no part in the peace talks, which he said would end by leaving his country permanently divided.

Later that day I wired Washington, and it was the first time the bears got into official correspondence. "Met for two hours with President Rhee," I telegraphed. "Foreign minister present plus two bears one of which nipped foreign minister. President Rhee opposes truce negotiations but will send observer to Panmunjom. President Rhee strongly urges us free Korean POWs. . . ."

I included the bears with the idea Washington probably needed cheering up, what with the venerable president's opposition to the armistice obviously making the task of negotiating that agreement no easier at Panmunjom, and also because I was repeating the message to Tokyo for

General Mark Wayne Clark, commander in chief of United Nations forces, who had just had an altercation with the foreign minister and flown back to Pershing Heights in his four-star airplane. Sure enough, the general called me early the next morning from Japan on my red-light army phone, an impressive experience that involved clearing the wires while the commanding general talked. Wayne Clark referred genially to the bears and then demanded how come I got on the subject of prisoners of war with the president of Korea since POWs were definitely *his* bailiwick.

I saw President Rhee's bears often thereafter, for the spring weather in Korea held fine and we met in the president's garden at Kyung MuDai, against the shoulder of North Mountain, while the jet planes from Kimpo screamed overhead and things moved slowly among the armistice negotiators. The two cubs had collars now and Captain Kwak used to lead them around the garden, each on a ten-foot chain, while they scuffled and batted each other across the lawn. And whenever they got free, which was almost once an afternoon, the bears either made for the tall cedar overlooking the goldfish pond, whereupon all negotiations stopped for the time it took Captain Kwak to get them down again, or else they made for the table under the wisteria arbor—the table around which we were sitting—whereat the foreign minister and I quickly got our feet off the ground while the president of Korea, looking benign, would relax and wait for Captain Kwak to get two collars back over four round black ears and lead the cubs away from us. Neither the foreign minister nor I ever figured out why the president didn't get nipped, but he never did and he never showed any nervousness when the two bears were romping around his shoelaces.

I don't remember when President Rhee decided to give the bears to President Eisenhower, but I do recall when he told me about it because it was at the end of an acrimonious session having to do with those same Korean prisoners of war, twenty-five thousand of whom President Rhee suddenly liberated, with spectacular results.

Since the Korean POWs were guarded by Republic of Korea troops, letting them out of their stockades was no difficult operation. The president called in his provost marshal, whose name was General Won Yung Duk, and instructed him to open the gates and invite the prisoners to come out, whereupon the ex-prisoners immediately merged with the rest of the Korean population. It was as simple as that, but it was also in contravention of the orders of the High Command, which took a very dim view of the arrangement.

The Communists also took a dim view of it, having other schemes in mind for war prisoners, and the Communists loudly charged bad faith, and accused us of collusion between the High Command and President Rhee. They threatened to terminate the armistice negotiations then and there, and we gathered that General Harrison, representing General Clark at Panmunjom, had an abrasive morning listening to the diatribes of General Nam Il and his *kimchi-*eating Chinese Communist colleagues.

Washington immediately ran a high fever, and General Clark and I were directed, in messages labeled NIACT (night action), to rally around and admonish President Rhee, whom we found in his Kyung MuDai garden, cheerfully unrepentant.

"What you do with the Chinese prisoners is no concern of mine," he told General Clark. "Also I am not concerned with the pro-Communist Koreans. But the others are anti-Communist Koreans, and they should have been released months ago. Now it is done."

As not infrequently happened, that stalwart patriot had the last word—since there was no possible way of rounding up the twenty-five thousand ex-prisoners of war—and presently Wayne Clark stalked out, six feet four of frustrated

general. The two bears were present, on leash, and General
Clark returned Captain Kwak's salute.

"About the bears," said the president amiably, as though
the bears had been the subject of all our previous discussion,
"I should like to give the bears to President Eisenhower. For
the Rock Creek Zoo. They will amuse the Washington children. Can you arrange to get them to Washington for me?"

I said I didn't know, but I'd be glad to find out, and I
added that the last presidential animals I had to do with
were a pair of pygmy hippos from Liberia that Harvey
Firestone wanted to give to President Coolidge. "Is that
so?" said President Rhee affably. "Well, anyway, the bears
probably aren't as big as even pygmy hippos, but they are
certainly growing." And we had tea together in the June sunshine of his garden.

By that time the two bears weighed forty and fifty
pounds, and they were in fact growing fast. I suspected that
they were eating the Rhees out of house and home, for the
president of Korea lived very frugally in his war-torn capital
and the upkeep of two hungry cubs must have been a
substantial item in his budget. The bears continued to grow,
and getting them to the Potomac turned out to be one of
the most protracted chores in diplomatic endeavor.

First I telegraphed Washington, citing my earlier message
about the foreign minister's having been nipped, because
bureaucrats always like to have something previous, tidily
of record, before they start thinking why a project is im-
practical. The State Department in due course replied,
informing me that the president would be pleased to accept
the bears and that the National Zoological Park was prepared to receive them. What kind of bears, the State Department inquired on behalf of the National Zoological Park,
were they? I replied that they were Korean bears, captured
the previous March on the east coast, over near the Sea
of Japan, and that they were black with white Vs on their

chests. (Turned out that the zoo identified them later as Himalayan bears, and was inclined to be churlish about my natural history. How Himalayan bears got to Korea is possibly another story.)

Having established the bears as *persona grata* to Washington, I tackled the Fifth Air Force, whose commanding general was a favorite of Mrs. Rhee. "Sam," I said, "the president wants to give his bear cubs to President Eisenhower for the Rock Creek Park Zoo. That's right—the bears that nipped the foreign minister. The zoo says its OK. So how's for some Air Force pressurized transportation from K-16 to the Potomac?"

Although for the foot soldiers the armistice negotiations had slowed down events along Porkchop Ridge and the Punch Bowl, the Fifth Air Force and the First Marine Air Wing were still plenty busy bombing bridges south of the Yalu, disrupting Communist communications, and chasing MIGs with their jets. Sam said so. He also recalled that President Roosevelt's son's dog, during World War II days, had attracted unfavorable attention from the press, when the dog came home by Air Force plane, allegedly displacing a sergeant.

I said I remembered President Roosevelt's son's dog, but I pointed out that the Fifth Air Force was moving one thousand American soldiers a day from Korea to Japan on R and R (rest and recreation), to say nothing of cargo planes coming to Seoul, one of which I hoped might be returning to the States with enough spare space for two now not so small bear cubs.

"I'll see what I can do," promised Sam.

There matters rested for several days, while the Communists at Panmunjom continued to heckle the United Nations Command over the liberated Korean war prisoners. And every time I saw the president he asked me how things, meaning the bears, were coming on. "How long," he asked, "did it take to get Mr. Firestone's pygmy hippos to Washington from Liberia?" I said the hippos came by ship.

Finally Sam phoned. "It's all set," he reported. "And I've lined up a couple of carpenters to make the crates. The plane leaves K-16 day after tomorrow."

I relayed the news to Kyung MuDai and President Rhee was pleased. "Kindly express my thanks to General Anderson," said the president. "I'll tell Captain Kwak to get ready."

"Captain Kwak," I said. "What about Captain Kwak, Mr. President?" "He has looked after them ever since they came to Kyung MuDai. He knows what they eat. It's a long trip to Washington. The bears would be lonely without him."

And that was that. Captain Kwak and the bear cubs were a package. No Captain Kwak, and the deal was off—which meant I still had the bears.

The Fifth Air Force was sympathetic, but equally firm. The Fifth Air Force would take the bear cubs, properly crated, and it would undertake to feed and water them en route, and to deliver them to National Airport in Washington. But it was sorry the Pentagon wouldn't approve transportation for a Korean policeman, and then be responsible for bringing him all the way back to Korea. Bears, yes; but Captain Kwak, no. The Air Force was sorry.

So Sam's plane took off without the bears, and I still had them. President Rhee was disappointed, and he said so.

Meanwhile the bears continued to grow. On July 27, the day the Korean armistice was finally signed, the bears celebrated the event by climbing the camouflage nets on the south side of the president's house. Furthermore the president didn't like the armistice any better as an accomplished fact than he had liked the armistice in prospect, and he threatened to resume fighting the Communists with the ROK Army.

It was at that point that the secretary of state of the United States decided to come from Washington to Korea.

He duly reached K-16, and on the way from the airport through the hot Korean night, I warned Mr. Dulles that if he didn't want two bear cubs for fellow passengers on the way back, plus one Korean policeman, the secretary of state had better be thinking of plausible reasons why he couldn't accommodate them.

The reply of the secretary of state indicated that he would be delighted to facilitate the gift to President Eisenhower, but if the bears got aboard his homeward-bound Constellation, one American ambassador would soon be out of a job.

Sure enough, during defense-pact negotiations the following day, the president turned to Mr. Dulles and said, "Mr. Secretary, I have two bear cubs that I'd like to give to President Eisenhower for the Rock Creek Zoo."

"That's fine," said the secretary genially. "I'm sure the president will be delighted." And Mr. Dulles shot a hard look at his ambassador to Korea.

"I've checked on that, Mr. President," said I. "Unfortunately the luggage compartment of the secretary's plane isn't pressurized, and they fly at over twenty thousand feet. I'm afraid the bears would find it pretty tough at that altitude."

So presently Secretary Dulles went away from Korea and I still had the two bears, not to forget Captain Kwak.

My next gambit was to tackle Northwest Airlines, which is the only American flag line serving Korea. Northwest was then engaged with the Ministry of Transportation, negotiating a transfer of its operations from Pusan, where they landed from Tokyo all during the Korean war, back to Seoul, the capital. I remembered that the president of Northwest, years ago when I was a vice consul in Peru, ran a cotton-dusting operation in the Cañete Valley. Later he ran PANAGRA, and during the war he saw distinguished service as a general in the Air Transport Command.

So I wrote to the president of Northwest Airlines, praising the bears, and recalling Old Times, and not forgetting Captain Kwak. I said the bears were tidy, sophisticated, and thoroughly photogenic, and that I was sure President Rhee would be glad to pose for photographs with them, and that the pilot could be photographed with them, and that doubtless Dr. Yang, the Korean ambassador to the United States, would be happy to be photographed at National Airport on the arrival of the bears and Captain Kwak in Washington. All to the prestige, I wrote, of Northwest Airlines.

I had a prompt and gratifying reply. Harold Harris said he'd be delighted to carry the bears, provided the Civil Aeronautics Board approved, and likewise to provide courtesy transportation for Captain Kwak—with or without photographs—and he was glad to know what diplomats in Korea did with their spare time when they weren't chasing pheasants or off duck shooting. As to official permission, the matter would have to be cleared with the Civil Aeronautics Board because common carriers were not allowed to provide gratis transportation except with the board's prior approval. A formality, no doubt, but would I please handle that matter with Washington?

My bear file was assuming substantial proportions, but I got off another cable to the State Department, summarizing developments and asking the State Department to obtain clearance from the Civil Aeronautics Board, which clearance I assumed would automatically be forthcoming.

Clearance was not automatically forthcoming. A week later I had in a message to the effect that the CAB viewed with disfavor free transportation in general, including bear cubs and Korean policemen. The State Department had endorsed my recommendation, but the board said no. The State Department said it was sorry; it suggested that perhaps the Air Force could provide transportation. . . .

It was now September, and I had been associated with

President Rhee's bears, in circumstances of increasing congestion, since the previous April.

Most of the time, when you are sitting at the far end of a cable circuit—in Zamboanga or Helsinki or Asunción or Seoul—a Foreign Service officer addresses himself with anonymous optimism to the secretary of state. Secstate, Washington, is the telegraphic symbol. So you dictate, "Secstate, Washington." And then you lay it on the line as articulately as you can, hoping that the problem as described eleven thousand miles from Foggy Bottom is going to make sense, if not to your titular chief, who is wrestling with High Policy and World Problems, at least to some diligent desk officer in his Virginia Avenue cubicle. That tired slave of the taxpayers holds your welfare in the hollow of his hand, and you hope he will earnestly get going on the solution of your problem before you perish on your distant dessicated vine, or start meeting little mauve men with triangular heads, oozing around the corner. Another remedy is a crock of square-shouldered Tennessee sour mash, but it is hard to come by where the pavement ends, and, with the Seventh Fleet moved down to Formosa, the American Embassy in Seoul was facing a Jack Daniels crisis.

"Secstate, Washington," I dictated. And then I had a vision of the foreign minister of Korea and me, with Captain Kwak on a leash, romping with President Rhee's two bears —now adult and full of teeth—all the way from Pusan to Munsan-ni, as long as I remained in Korea. "Secstate, Washington," I repeated. And then I added that the message was personal, for a distinguished public servant who accompanied the secretary of state when Mr. Dulles came to Seoul with our mutual defense pact. I named that public servant.

"Re President Rhee's bears," I dictated. "CAB says Northwest Airlines which represents important American interest in Korea, and has offered transport bears Washington as goodwill gesture, cannot, repeat not, provide gratis transportation from Seoul. Paragraph. When President Rhee four months ago asked me arrange send bears Washington as gift to President U.S. bears weighed 30 pounds each. They now weigh 150 pounds. Paragraph. Bears are still growing."

Two days later the Northwest Airlines manager in Tokyo phoned me to say the deal was approved in Washington. An official telegram confirmed it. We picked a fine September afternoon for the departure of the bears from Seoul, and the pictures in the garden at Kyung MuDai constitute a permanent record. There were brown pods on the wisteria vine and the bumblebees had disappeared, along with the foreign minister. The two bears looked very handsome posing with President Rhee and Captain Kwak, who wore a fine new black serge uniform with the insignia and gold buttons of the Korean police.

Captain Kwak returned to Seoul two weeks later, with pictures of Ambassador Yang and the bears at the Washington airport. And always thereafter, when I called at Kyung MuDai in the shadow of North Mountain, Captain Kwak opened the presidential door for me, and he invariably saluted.

Set in Caledonia, Clarendon, and Commercial Script type faces by the Vail-Ballou Press and Philmac Typographers. Frontispiece and jacket in full color reproduced by the Capper Engraving Co. Reproduction of the drawings and printing of the text by The Murray Printing Co. Paper specially made by the Curtis Paper Co. for Whitehead & Alliger. Binding by the H. Wolff Book Manufacturing Co.